So, You Want to Be Like Christ?

So, You Want to Be Like Christ?

Eight Essentials To Get You There

CHARLES R. SWINDOLL

Published by
THOMAS NELSON
Since 1798
www.thomasnelson.com

With great love and deep respect,
I dedicate this book to my granddaughter,

HEATHER NELSON.

Even though only sixteen years old,
Heather wants to be like Christ
as much as anyone I know—
in fact, more than most I know.

Published in Nashville, Tennessee 37214, by Thomas Nelson, Inc.

Published in association with Yates & Yates, LLP, Attorneys and Counselors, Orange, California

Thomas Nelson, Inc. books may be purchased in bulk for educational, business, fundraising, or sales promotional use. For information, please email SpecialMarkets@ThomasNelson.com.

All Scripture quotations, unless otherwise indicated, are taken from the New American Standard Bible (NASB). Copyright © 1960, 1962, 1963, 1968, 1971, 1973, 1975, 1977 by The Lockman Foundation, La Habra, California. Used by permission.

Other Scripture references are from the following sources:
    The New King James Version (NKJV), copyright © 1979, 1980, 1982, Thomas Nelson, Inc., Publishers.
    THE AMPLIFIED BIBLE (Amp.), Old Testament copyright © 1965, 1987 by the Zondervan Corporation. The Amplified New Testament copyright © 1958, 1987 by the Lockman Foundation. Used by permission.
    The NET Bible ® (NET) copyright © 2003 by Biblical Studies Press, L.L.C. www.netbible.com All rights reserved. Used by permission.
    The Moffatt Bible (MOFFAT), copyright © 1913, 1924.

ISBN 13: 978-0-8499-1352-5 (tradepaper)
ISBN 0-8499-1731-X (hardcover)

Printed in the United States of America
09 10 11 12 13   RRD   16 15 14 13 12

Contents

Acknowledgments

No book worth reading is the result of only one person's work. It is the combined effort of many that enhances the final product, as each contributor adds his or her expertise to the process.

Mike Hyatt of Thomas Nelson Publishers and David Moberg of W Publishing Group first urged me to write on this subject. I have both of them to thank for their encouragement, commitment, and loyal friendship through many years.

I also express my profound appreciation to the one with whom I have worked the closest, Mark Gaither, who has taken my original words (usually handwritten) and breathed fresh life into them with his editorial skills and creative turn of a phrase. Thanks, Mark, for a job very well done!

And finally, I must mention my longtime friend Mary Hollingsworth, along with her outstanding staff of fellow workers at Shady Oaks Studio. Mary and her efficient team not only provided much-needed attention to detail in editing and putting the finishing touches on the final copy of my manuscript, but they also researched and secured all the rights and approvals to the quotations and other illustrative material I have used in each chapter.

Hats off to all of you fine folks who have worked behind the scenes, seeing this volume to completion. My gratitude to each of you knows no bounds.

Introduction:
The Gymnasium of the Soul

I had the great privilege of getting to know the late coach of the Dallas Cowboys, Tom Landry, while he served on the Dallas Theological Seminary board. He was a humble man of quiet strength and dignity, and when he chose to say something, an entire room would stop and lean in to hear what he had to say. Once during a breakfast with a group of men, someone asked how he was able to forge a team out of individuals so that they would win, something he managed to do every year for twenty-nine years. I'll never forget his answer. The table grew silent as he paused for a moment, and then said, "My job is to get men to do what they don't want to do in order to achieve what they've always wanted to achieve."

The something that those men wanted to achieve was a victory at the Super Bowl. What they didn't want to do was the grueling work it would take to get them there. Achieving anything requires discipline—determined, deliberate, definable actions with a clear goal in mind. A good coach will help the team achieve its goal by outlining the exercises and motivating the players to stick to the plan. Facilitating and encouraging discipline in order to win—that's what coaching is all about. With your permission, I hope to do a little of that in this book.

Tom Landry was distinctive in one other respect. In a professional league led predominately by overweight coaches—many just one cheese fry away from a major heart attack—Coach Landry looked like he could still suit up and play. Well into his sixties, he never asked his team to do anything he wasn't willing to do. What I want to share with you in the pages that follow are insights, perspectives, and strategies that I have developed during my years in ministry. Some come naturally now. Others still require all the discipline I can muster. But in every case, I can honestly say that I am more consistent now than last year, and vastly improved over my rookie season. In short, I suggest nothing in this book that I don't require of myself.

Many centuries ago, Paul coached Timothy, his son in the ministry, with the words, "Discipline yourself for the purpose of godliness" (1 Timothy 4:7). Timothy was the pastor of the church in Ephesus, a Las Vegas sort of city near the Mediterranean coast in present-day Turkey. This city was a busy cosmopolitan crossroad, buzzing with the commerce of a world empire. It was a judicial sanctuary for criminals and hucksters awaiting trial. The temple of Artemis—one of the wonders of the ancient world—drew worshippers from every corner of the empire, which created a volatile mix of the occult and money. Ephesus was a busy, rich, sensual place to be a Christian. Sound familiar?

Paul wanted his son in the ministry to be a good servant of Jesus Christ as he coached others in the same way he had been coached, nourishing himself on the words of the faith and sound doctrine

(v. 6). But the apostle knew by his own experience that it wouldn't be automatic, it wouldn't be easy, and it doesn't come quickly, especially in a place like Ephesus. Timothy would need to discipline himself.

Discipline. Such a hard word to read, isn't it? It drips with sweat. So unpleasant. It calls to mind those grueling days I spent in boot camp after I joined the Marine Corps. I also think of the endless hours a football player must endure on the practice field and in the weight room. When I see the word *discipline,* I think of punishing workouts that produce results everyone admires . . . and no one enjoys.

Then when I see the word applied to the Christian life, I think, *Oh, Great. That's all I need is another chore!* So in writing a book on the "spiritual disciplines," I run the risk of standing in line behind your dentist, who scolds you for not flossing, and your cardiologist, who callously pokes your expanding gut. I don't want to shame you into walking a spiritual treadmill, nor do I want to convince you that a no-fun checklist of spiritual tedium will somehow pay dividends in eternity. On the other hand, I don't want to suggest that becoming like Christ will be easy. Seeking intimacy with the Almighty requires focused determination, demands specific changes in attitude and behavior, and will come with a number of heartbreak and setbacks.

In other words, I'm not selling an exercise program. I'm not asking you to turn a new leaf starting with this book. This is merely an invitation to live life as Christ intended, which includes difficult choices, some hard work, and an increasing capacity to enjoy all the goodness God offers those who come to Him.

Paul chose carefully when he selected the Greek term *gumnazo.* (Most English transliterations spell it *gymnazo,* from which we get our word *gymnasium.*) The New American Standard Bible renders it "discipline." Look at how several other translations present Paul's command:

Keep yourself in training for a godly life. (GNT)
Exercise yourself toward godliness. (NKJV)
Exercise daily in God—no spiritual flabbiness, please! (MSG)
Train yourself for godliness. (NET Bible)
Train yourself to be godly. (NIV)
Spend your time and energy in training yourself for spiritual fitness. (NLT)
Take the time and trouble to keep yourself spiritually fit. (Phillips)

Paul has in mind the word picture of an athlete preparing for the day of competition. I would prefer to translate it "Condition yourself," which raises two points:

First, conditioning involves repetitive training exercises so that the athlete's mind and the appropriate muscle groups learn to work together reflexively and automatically. Conditioning combines endurance and skill. Conditioning turns game-winning abilities into habits.

Second, no one can condition someone else. An athlete can seek out a coach to help him with conditioning, but he cannot hire someone to do the work for him. Condition *yourself.* Check the Internet, look through the *Yellow Pages.* If you ever find "Lease-a-Dieter" or "Rent-a-Runner," let me know. I want the number!

Conditioning is between you and God.

Notice also that Paul has a goal in mind for the conditioning. Runners condition themselves by running. Weightlifters condition themselves by lifting weights. Each trains for a specific skill to compete in a specific event. Paul's event is godliness. "Condition yourself toward godliness." Paul uses the Greek word for godliness ten times in his writings; eight of them appear in 1 Timothy. Godliness is central to Paul's advice to Timothy.

Introduction

Ask people around the coffee pot at work what "godliness" means and see what kind of answers you get. Some picture a monk removed from the challenges of the world, studying, praying, meditating, humming hymns behind the walls of a monastery. Others see a squeaky-clean, Bible-toting, do-gooder. Naïve, moralistic . . . annoyingly innocent. One scholar defines the word this way:

> Christian [godliness] is not moralistic, for it is rooted in the Christ event (1 Timothy 3:16). It is not just outward worship, nor a mere concept of God, nor a virtue, nor an ideal. Over against a [Gnostic philosophy of self-deprivation] that regards creation as bad . . . true [godliness], born of faith, covers everyday conduct in honoring God as Creator and Redeemer, even though it may expect persecution from the very orders of God which it respects.[1]

A "godly" person is one who ceases to be *self*-centered in order to become *God*-centered. Christ became a man and, as a result of His earthly ministry, we see how God intended for humans to behave. Jesus is our unblemished example of godliness. Therefore, a godly person is a Christlike person.

Our goal as Christians is to become like Christ.

Some well-meaning, yet tragically misguided leaders seem to think that becoming like Christ means that we should strive to be perfect . . . like Christ. For them, the disciplines are like pushups and sit-ups, spiritual exercises to beat their bodies and minds into submission. They'll even twist Paul's use of that image in 1 Corinthians 9:27 to make their point. Unfortunately, they are more Gnostic than Christian. While master of the body is important, and spiritual calisthenics *will* make the soul stronger, these are minor issues when it comes to the Christian view of spiritual activity. If you merely want to have more control over your lusts, or become more serene, any meditative religion will do.

Christianity and its goal, Christlikeness, have a person in mind: Christ! What sets Christian spiritual activity apart from all other religions is that they have knowledge of Christ as their goal; not moral perfection (although you will become more moral), not tranquility (although your life will become remarkably more peaceful). And because of the grace you have in Christ, the disciplines will do nothing to make you more accepted by the Father. You cannot be more accepted than you already are in Christ, since He has already done it all for you!

So why exercise spiritual disciplines? To know Jesus Christ. They are simply a means by which you come to know Him experientially. By imitating Him, by sharing His experiences, by living life as He lived it, allowing the Holy Spirit to shape you by the disciplines from the inside out, you will become more like Him.

Don't believe me? Look at how Paul described his spiritual activity to the church in Philippi. This will be a key verse for us. We'll return to it often to remind us of the goal—why we are doing the things we're doing.

[For my determined purpose is] that I may know Him—that I may progressively become more deeply and intimately acquainted with Him, perceiving and recognizing and understanding [the wonders of His Person] more strongly and more clearly, and that I may in that same way come to know the power outflowing from His resurrection [which it exerts over believers]; and that I may so share His sufferings as to be continually transformed [in spirit into His likeness even] to His death, (Philippians 3:10, The Amplified Bible, Expanded Edition)

When you pray, pray so that you may know Him. When you seek to simplify, do it as a means of knowing Him more. When you surrender, or behave with humility or sacrifice, do it with the sole purpose in mind to know Him.

As you read the following chapters, keep in mind that each "essential" that I present is both a means *and* an end. Each is a distinctive mark of godliness that Christ modeled with perfection and, for that reason, each is worth imitating. Do them, and you will be like Christ. But they are also a means to knowing Him. For instance, intimacy with the Almighty, the subject of our first chapter, is the focus of all Christian activity—including those beyond the handful I discuss in this book. But intimacy is also the means by which we achieve our ultimate objective: transformation to His likeness. This is our primary goal, isn't it?

So, you want to be like Christ? Me too. But that kind of godliness won't just happen by hanging around a church or thinking lofty thoughts three or four times a day or learning a few verses of Scripture. It will take more—much more. Disciplining ourselves will require the same kind of focused thinking and living that our Master modeled during His brief life on earth.

Everything starts in the gymnasium of the soul. Since this is true, let's commit ourselves to these eight spiritual disciplines. I am now convinced that they are essential ways to help us get there. To borrow words from Coach Landry, these disciplines will enable us to do what we don't want to do in order to achieve what we've always wanted to achieve.

—CHUCK SWINDOLL
Dallas, Texas

Intimacy:

Deepening Our Lives

We live in a society that tries to diminish us to the level of the antheap so that we scurry mindlessly, getting and consuming. It is essential to take counteraction. . . . Every one of us needs to be stretched to live at our best, awakened out of dull moral habits, shaken out of petty and trivial busy-work.[1]

—EUGENE PETERSON

Intimacy:

Deepening Our Lives

Several years ago my wife and I took a journey. We traveled 250 miles south and over forty years back in time—back to Houston, Texas. Our roots run deep there. Roots that are personal and, in many ways, spiritual. Decades had passed since our last visit, so we were in for a lot of surprises.

We drove by houses where each of us had once lived and high schools we had attended. We did it slowly, revisiting the years that fill our memories. Everything felt so much smaller. If you've ever traced your roots, lingering over places steeped in nostalgia, you know what I mean.

My boyhood home on Quince Street, on the east side of Houston, was tiny compared to the memories I keep. I remember scootin' down that sidewalk toward the Methodist church on a skateboard scooter I made from scrap lumber and a roller skate that had lost its mate. As we drove to the end of the street, I remembered endless days of my boyhood playing sandlot football with Bruce and a bunch of buddies. I swelled with pride any time he picked me to be on his team, because if

3

you were on Bruce's team, you always won. I realize now that Bruce was a high school dropout who just hung around the vacant lot at the end of Quince to play football. He probably should have been in college when most of us were in ninth or tenth grade. But at the time, none of that mattered. I just remember the fun we had throwing passes and having Bruce lead the blocking as I carried the football across the goal line of that sandy lot with odd patches of grass growing here and there.

I drove the route from our home on Quince Street to Milby High School, and I recalled what a martyr I thought I was for having to walk that distance. It's only about a ten-block stroll, but back then it seemed much farther.

Cynthia's childhood memories took her through a junior high school and then her years rooting for the fighting Yellow Jackets of Galena Park High School. She, too, lived near her school. She remembered her classmates, the school chorale, boys she dated, and church activities she faithfully attended. We laughed and sighed together as we dug our way through those years when life moved slowly and days were simple and easygoing.

We lingered in front of the first little house she and I bought for $9,995. It was a brand-new framed house in Channelview, a suburb of Houston. We sat in front of churches where we had once worshiped and served. We drove through neighborhoods where we had grown up as we followed roads we had traveled before meeting each other and then later as a young married couple.

The whole time we reminisced over friends we knew, stores where we shopped, neighbors we liked, and decisions we made. We recalled celebrations and tragedies we had shared, pain we had known, and the many joys that healed them for both of us. So many of those places that time had now passed by were meaningful to us. We were there again, feeling those long-ago feelings. Familiar, yet very strange. They were

4

random remnants of experiences created by
what felt like a different Chuck and Cynthia.

As we pulled away and I watched the places
of our memories disappear in my rearview
mirror, Cynthia and I came upon two giant
realizations.

First, *how necessary is change*. We're so grateful
we're not where we once were more than fifty
years ago, not only geographically but also spiritually and personally. Growth *is* change but, as
we will see later, not all change is growth.

Growth is change, but as we will see later, not all change is growth.

Second, *how essential is perspective*. Life seemed so complicated, so
difficult while living it back then. But glancing back over our shoulders, more than five decades down a highway leading away from
Houston, things looked very different because *we* were different.

GROWING BEYOND EARLY LOVE VERSUS LEAVING IT

Let's shift gears from the geographical and the physical realms to the
spiritual and the personal. In doing so, let me remind you of an ancient
church that you and I would probably have attended had we lived in
that city at the end of the first century. It was among the best churches
of that era. The church is named simply "the church in Ephesus"
(Revelation 2:1). This is what the Lord Himself had to say about this
church as He sized it up:

> I know your deeds and your toil and perseverance, and that you
> cannot tolerate evil men, and you put to the test those who call them-
> selves apostles, and they are not, and you found them to be false.
>
> —REVELATION 2:2

Here is a church that worked diligently and was known for its zeal and discernment. They would have nothing to do with apostolic pretenders. This discerning group of believers formed a church famous for its doctrine. It was biblically sound and probably had strong leaders, with many courageous people willing to take a stand in opposition to wrong. They gave no time to folks who were phony. They were zealous and firm and relentless in their pursuit of truth. So far, so good. Who can argue with orthodoxy? However, all was not well in the Ephesian church.

Verse 4 begins with what linguists call a particle of contrast: *but*. For three verses we read of nothing but commendable things, attributes of a local assembly of believers that would have drawn you and hundreds of other first-century worshipers like you to the church at Ephesus. "But I have this against you," the Lord says with a sigh. "You have left your first love."

A. T. Robertson, in his *Word Pictures in the New Testament*, writes, "This early love, proof of the new life in Christ . . . had cooled off in spite of their doctrinal purity. They had remained orthodox, but had become unloving."[2]

John R. W. Stott, in a small but wonderful work entitled *What Christ Thinks of the Church*, adds these thoughts about the Ephesian believers:

> They had fallen from the early heights of devotion to Christ which they had climbed. They had descended to the plains of mediocrity. In a word, they were backsliders. . . . Certainly the hearts of the Ephesian Christians had chilled.[3]

I can't speak for you, but it puts a shiver up my back when I see the word *chilled*. What an indictment! What a horrible way to describe the heart of a Christian! I think of death when I hear that word used to describe a heart.

A little later Stott continues, "Their first flush of ecstasy had passed. Their early devotion to Christ had cooled. They had been in love with Him, but they had fallen out of love."[4]

How much had changed since Paul had penned his last comment to that church in his letter to the Ephesians: "Grace be with all those who love our Lord Jesus Christ *with incorruptible love*" (Ephesians 6:24, emphasis added).

In that benediction, I feel a longing in the great apostle's heart that the Ephesian Christians experience no waning of love. By the time John wrote the book of Revelation thirty years later, Paul's dreams were dashed. Jesus said, in effect, "You left that love. You once had a love that was incorruptible, but you abandoned it. You once enjoyed a devotion that was consistent, meaningful, satisfying. In fact, the warmth of your love transformed your thinking and your attitudes; it revolutionized the way you related to Me, to your heavenly Father, and to your brothers and sisters. But you have cooled off."

John Stott aptly portrays the scene:

> The tide of devotion had turned and was ebbing fast. They toiled with vigour, but not with love. They endured with fortitude but without love. They tested their teachers with orthodoxy but had no love in their hearts.[5]

Just as Cynthia and I returned to our roots and came away with a valuable perspective, I invite you to do that now. It won't take long. The mind is an amazing thing. In a matter of seconds, your mind can transport you to scenes you thought you had forgotten. And all it takes is a little bit of time and some honest reflection. Cynthia and I did it again and again as we drove by the familiar haunts of our childhood, teenage, and young adult years.

Let's go on a brief spiritual pilgrimage together.

Journey back in your mind to your first days as a brand-new believer in Jesus Christ. Return to that time when your love was budding and emerging into full bloom. Remember when you would speak of Christ and it would ignite your heart with an exciting burst of zeal and delight? Remember when prayer was new and untried, and you felt its power as you communed with the Almighty? Remember when the Bible was that delicious Book of truth filled with delectable insights you had never known before? Remember when sharing Him with someone else represented the highlight of your week? Remember when your devotion was consistent, fulfilling, enriching . . . deep?

What happened to all of that? When you ponder those questions—not just in passing, but taking time to concentrate as you ponder them—perhaps you feel like one of the Ephesian Christians whom Jesus urged, "Remember from where you have fallen, and repent and do the deeds you did at first" (Revelation 2:5).

Remember, we said earlier that growth is change, but not all change is growth. Cynthia and I would never choose to return to those early days, not even to when our love was in springtime, delightfully new and fresh. Those were wonderful days and wonderful feelings, but our love has grown. The love we enjoy now is deeper, characterized by a comfortable ease and a profound sense of security that nearly fifty years of life shared together has earned.

Not so for the Ephesians! And perhaps not so for you in your relationship with God. Look again at what Jesus commanded. Your spiritual life may be in need of some major changes. A new perspective is essential in order to rekindle that first-love kind of relationship where God is real again, where you and He are on much closer speaking terms. The kind of intimacy that doesn't require a stirring message from the pulpit and doesn't depend upon a great worship event or concert but simply exists as a natural part of your walk.

INTIMACY WITH GOD REQUIRES ACTION

Distance from God is a frightening thing. God will never adjust His agenda to fit ours. He will not speed His pace to catch up with ours; we need to slow *our* pace in order to recover our walk with Him. God will not scream and shout over the noisy clamor; He expects us to seek quietness, where His still, small voice can be heard again. God will not work within the framework of our complicated schedules; we must adapt to His style. We need to conform to His way if our lives are to be characterized by the all-encompassing word *godliness.*

*D*istance from God is a frightening thing. God will never adjust His agenda to fit ours.

Godliness is still our desire as believers, isn't it?

But the great question is, how? How do busy people, living fast-paced and complicated lives, facing relentless pressures, consistently walk with God? Whatever would be included in the answers, we can be assured that they will not come naturally, automatically, quickly, or easily. I do not think a person on this earth has ever been automatically godly or quickly godly or easily and naturally godly. "This world is no friend of grace to help us on to God."[6] Everything around us is designed to make us dissatisfied with our present condition.

Henri Nouwen said that while he was driving through Los Angeles on one occasion, he felt like he was driving through a giant dictionary—words everywhere, sounds everywhere, signs everywhere, saying, "Use me, take me, buy me, drink me, smell me, touch me, kiss me, sleep with me."[7] He found himself longing to get away from all those words, all those giant signs and sounds. Why? Not because there was something innately wrong with those things—some, but not all. He grieved that it was all so empty, so devoid of God.

So how do we pull it off? How, in a world bent on distracting us from growing deeper in our first love, always enticing us to pursue the pointless, do we find closeness with God? How do you and I become more godly?

This question has led me back to a word that I used much more in my early days in ministry than I have in recent years. The word is *discipline*. The secret lies in our returning to the spiritual disciplines.

DISCIPLINE YOURSELF FOR INTIMACY WITH GOD

Pause long enough to read the following scripture slowly. It is Paul's advice to Timothy, his son in the faith:

> But the Spirit explicitly says that in later times some will fall away from the faith, paying attention to deceitful spirits and doctrines of demons, by means of the hypocrisy of liars seared in their own conscience as with a branding iron, men who forbid marriage and advocate abstaining from foods which God has created to be gratefully shared in by those who believe and know the truth. For everything created by God is good, and nothing is to be rejected if it is received with gratitude; for it is sanctified by means of the word of God and prayer.
>
> In pointing out these things to the brethren, you will be a good servant of Christ Jesus, constantly nourished on the words of the faith and of the sound doctrine which you have been following. But have

nothing to do with worldly fables fit only for old women. *On the other hand, discipline yourself for the purpose of godliness;* for bodily discipline is only of little profit, but godliness is profitable for all things, since it holds promise for the present life and also for the life to come.

—1 TIMOTHY 4:1–8, emphasis added

Paul was sitting alone in a dungeon when he wrote this letter to Timothy. His younger friend was serving as the pastor of a church—interestingly, the church in Ephesus. This instruction came sometime after the letter Paul wrote to the Ephesians and before the letter Jesus wrote to that same church in Revelation 2.

Consider Eugene Peterson's paraphrase of that passage in *The Message:*

The Spirit makes it clear that as time goes on, some are going to give up on the faith and chase after demonic illusions put forth by professional liars. These liars have lied so well and for so long that they've lost their capacity for truth. They will tell you not to get married. They'll tell you not to eat this or that food—perfectly good food God created to be eaten heartily and with thanksgiving by Christians! Everything God created is good, and to be received with thanks. Nothing is to be sneered at and thrown out. God's Word and our prayers make every item in creation holy.

You've been raised on the Message of the faith and have followed sound teaching. Now pass on this counsel to the Christians there, and you'll be a good servant of Jesus. Stay clear of silly stories that get dressed up as religion. Exercise daily in God—no spiritual flabbiness, please! Workouts in the gymnasium are useful, but a disciplined life in God is far more so, making you fit both today and forever.

—1 TIMOTHY 4:1–8 MSG

I think verse 7 represents the climax of Paul's instruction to Timothy. Don't miss this advice: "Discipline yourself for the purpose of godliness." In other words, "Timothy, get serious about your walk with God! It's time to step up, young man . . . godliness won't *just happen.*"

*I*t is so easy to get religious instead of godly.

Guess what, churchgoing men and women: religion won't cut it! We live in a spiritual hothouse where we talk religious talk and send religious letters and write religious pamphlets and do religious Bible study guides and answer religious phones (religiously) and deal with religious concerns. It is so easy to get religious instead of godly. And all the while, a chilling religion slowly cools our hearts. Ironic, isn't it? The general public may have this marvelous idea about how godly we are, when if the truth were known, many of us would have to say, "I am stagnant, and I have been that way longer than I want to admit."

What's missing? Stop and think. It's that "first love," the great fountain that both generates the spiritual disciplines and feeds on them. Yet I find it absolutely amazing that in the process of doing spiritual things (not religious things, but truly *spiritual* things), we can fail to "discipline" ourselves "for the purpose of godliness." I can, and I have.

Therefore in recent months I have sensed a genuine need—in my own life first (before I ever speak or write to someone else, I have to address it in my own life)—for the cultivation of intimacy with the Almighty. Those words are carefully chosen. They are put forth in deliberate contrast. The almighty, awesome God loves it when we are intimate with Him. So, our goal is intimacy, and, according to Scripture, intimacy with God requires spiritual disciplines. In this book I will address eight disciplines that are essential in our pursuit of godliness.

INTIMACY WITH GOD CULTIVATES WISDOM

While rummaging through an old bookstore some time ago, I came across Dallas Willard's excellent work *The Spirit of the Disciplines*. Bedside reading, it is not. This convicting piece of literature is not something you plop down on the sofa and read alongside *People* magazine. Willard's words require you to think with him. For example:

> The modern age is an age of revolution—revolution motivated by insight into the appalling vastness of human suffering and need. Pleas for holiness and attacks on sin and Satan were used for centuries as the guide and the cure for the human situation. Today such pleas have been replaced with a new agenda. On the communal level, political and social critiques yield recipes for revolutions meant to liberate humankind from its many bondages. And on the individual level various self-fulfillment techniques promise personal revolutions bringing "freedom in an unfree world" and passage into the good life. Such are modern answers to humanity's woes.
>
> Against this background a few voices have continued to emphasize that the cause of the distressed human condition, individual and social—and its only possible cure—is a *spiritual* one. But what these voices are saying is not clear. They point out that social and political revolutions have shown no tendency to transform the heart of darkness that lies deep in the breast of every human being. That is evidently true. And amid a flood of techniques for self-fulfillment there is an epidemic of depression, suicide, personal emptiness, and escapism through drugs and alcohol, cultic obsession, consumerism, and sex and violence—all combined with an inability to sustain deep and enduring personal relationships.
>
> So obviously the problem *is* a spiritual one. And so must be the cure.

But if the cure is spiritual, how does modern Christianity fit into the answer? Very poorly, it seems, for Christians are among those caught up in the sorrowful epidemic just referred to. And that fact is so prominent that modern thinking has come to view the Christian faith as powerless, even somehow archaic, at the very least irrelevant. . . .

There is a deep longing among Christians and non-Christians alike for the personal purity and power to live as our hearts tell us we should. What we need is a deeper insight into our practical relationship with God in redemption. We need an understanding that can guide us into constant interaction with the Kingdom of God as a real part of our daily lives.[8]

"The Kingdom of God as a real part of our daily lives." I want that. I want that for you more than any other thing. I want that for every soul reading this book. But the hardest thing in the world, it seems, is for God to have our full attention so that intimacy with Him glows from within and can be seen by others as a passion that is authentic. He

I want fulfillment in my walk with Christ, not just talk about fulfillment.

wants no mere show of religion but a passionate spirituality, where God still does miraculous things through His people—often in spite of us—where God reveals His will in ways that are full of mystery and surprise and wonder. A humble spirituality that leaves us, the clay, willingly soft and malleable in the hands of the Potter, our sovereign God. I repeat, I want that for me and I want that for you.

Again and again and again the words *deep* and *deeper* appear in Willard's book. I want depth; I don't want heights. I want substance; I don't want speed. I want fulfillment in my walk with Christ, not just talk about fulfillment. I want to be able to think theologically and biblically, not be entertained with theological theories and biblical stories. I believe *you* want that, too, or you wouldn't be reading these pages.

Richard Foster's meaningful work *Celebration of Discipline* includes these words: "Superficiality is the curse of our age. The doctrine of instant satisfaction is a primary spiritual problem. The desperate need today is not for a greater number of intelligent people, or gifted people, but for deep people."[9]

Don't suspect for a moment that our environment makes us deep. In my current involvement at Dallas Seminary, I can be as superficial and shallow as a man could be and still be the chancellor of that great school, lacking depth all the while. Hanging out at church hoping it will transform you into a deep Christian is only slightly less foolish than expecting enough time in a garage to turn you into a car. Our environment—even a spiritually nurturing one—won't change us. The Spirit of God working on our volition changes us. Furthermore I am now convinced that we become more malleable in the hands of the Spirit when softened by the disciplines. Inevitably God works through those disciplines to create people with depth—people with a greater capacity for wisdom.

WITH WISDOM COMES CHRISTLIKENESS

We need wisdom, not just knowledge. God is willing to give wisdom, but not on our terms. As we go deeper, He begins to entrust us with more and more of His mind. In the process we become more and more like Christ.

When tragedy strikes, we don't need more intelligence. We don't need a greater number of skills. We need depth, the kind of depth Job had. When the bottom dropped out of his life, Job had the wisdom to say:

> But He knows the way I take;
> When He has tried me, I shall come forth as gold.
> My foot has held fast to His path;
> I have kept His way and not turned aside.
> I have not departed from the command of His lips;
> I have treasured the words of His mouth more than my necessary food.
>
> —JOB 23:10–12

We need the depth of Paul, who, after praying three times for the horrible stake in his flesh to leave (the word often translated "thorn" means a pointed instrument, like a sword), and three times the Lord said no. In response, Paul said, "Most gladly I will rather boast in my infirmities, that the power of Christ may rest upon me" (2 Corinthians 12:9 NKJV). That's depth. That's an example of wisdom at work. Rather than throw a pity party for himself, Paul boldly declared, "I choose to embrace my affliction so that I can have the privilege of experiencing even more of Christ's power over me."

What depth of character. What intimacy with the Almighty these men had. I want that too. I want what they had, so that my walk is such that I walk in step whether I feel good or not. Whether I get a yes or no to my prayers, I walk consistently, even when I don't get my own way.

WISDOM IS CULTIVATED ON GOD'S TERMS, NOT OURS

God often does His best work in us when He catches us by surprise and introduces a change that is completely against our own desire.

A couple of years after Cynthia and I were married, I had an obligation to fulfill in the military, so I joined the Marine Corps. I endured boot camp and advanced infantry training, which I completed at Camp Pendleton. I then received orders to serve my tour of duty in San Francisco. Cynthia and I were elated. Other guys were going to hot deserts, like Barstow, California, and lonely places like Okinawa, out in the middle of nowhere. Some were assigned to guard duty aboard a ship and would have to be at sea for six months at a time.

Not me. My assigned duty was at 100 Harrison Street in San Francisco, an enviable, plum assignment. We bought a new car and took off on our first road trip through the Sierras to that beautiful and romantic city on the California peninsula. It was fabulous! While we were settling into our little studio apartment in Daly City, we got connected with a fine church located south of us, Peninsula Bible Church. That's where I met Ray Stedman for the first time. I even attended a Bible conference at Mount Hermon. Two years into marriage, everything was working and life was charming. Candidly, we had it made.

Then . . . an unexpected letter came in the mail. At first I didn't even bother to open it; it was one of those form letters the military sends out by the truckloads. I sat staring out into the San Francisco bay in front of a little electronics firm waiting for Cynthia to finish work. I could see Alcatraz, straight ahead. Eventually I pulled the letter out of my pocket, sliced it open, and immediately noticed the printed signature at the bottom: Dwight D. Eisenhower, the president. It was a speed letter containing the official order for me to change from San Francisco to Okinawa. And, of course, I did what anybody would have done. I checked the envelope to make sure it was sent to the right person. No mistake. It was mine. Immediately my whole frame of reference changed.

Cynthia and I wept ourselves to sleep that night. Early on in our marriage, that tour of duty would take me sixty-five hundred miles away from her for no fewer than sixteen months. It felt like our world had spun off its axis and come to an end.

What I considered to be the most God-awful letter became the most God-ordained statement for me.

Little did I realize how that one small sheet of paper would change my entire life. What I considered to be the most God-awful letter became the most God-ordained statement for me. It opened doors I would never have otherwise passed through. It forced me out of my familiar, somewhat pampered existence and into a world of stretching opportunities that laid the groundwork for a ministry I would never have known or pursued. But at that moment—the moment it began—I could not imagine anything good coming from such a shocking disappointment.

Before I left, my brother shoved a book in my hand titled *Through Gates of Splendor*, the story of five missionaries who were martyred in Ecuador and their widows, who went on to evangelize the same Auca Indians who had murdered their husbands. On that troop ship, during the seventeen days between California and Okinawa, I discovered a whole new frame of reference. For the first time since I received the speed letter, my mind stopped resisting. For the first time I stopped focusing on myself. For the first time I began to think, *Maybe there's a divine plan at work here.*

I met a man named Bob Newkirk on the island of Okinawa. And one of the first things Bob gave me was a newly released translation of the New Testament—really, a paraphrase—called the *Amplified New Testament*. When I opened to read that paraphrase of the Scriptures for the first time, I found that Bob had marked only one verse: Philippians 3:10. I read that volume through at least three times before I left the island, but this verse kept coming back to me:

[For my determined purpose is] that I may know Him—that I may progressively become more deeply and intimately acquainted with Him, perceiving and recognizing and understanding [the wonders of His Person] more strongly and more clearly, and that I may in that same way come to know the power outflowing from His resurrection [which it exerts over believers]; and that I may so share His sufferings as to be continually transformed [in spirit into His likeness even] to His death.

—PHILIPPIANS 3:10 AMP

That's it! That's why I wound up on Okinawa! Humanly speaking, I never would have met Bob Newkirk in the safe haven of Houston or during our idyllic honeymoon in San Francisco. But halfway around the world, away from all the crutches, separated from all of those things that made me comfortable, I was given a chance to see God at work cross-culturally like never before. And the government paid my way! For the first time I would spend time in a missionary home. For the first time I would be surrounded by another culture and baffled by another language. For the first time in my life *I* would be the foreigner. And I found myself again and again and again having to look to heaven and learn a whole new way of walking. And best of all, my first love really began to bloom.

"My determined purpose [perhaps Paul means 'my focus'] is *that I may know Him.*

INTIMACY WITH GOD MUST BE INTENTIONAL

I will be using two important terms that need defining as we move through the chapters that follow. The first is *intimacy*. The second is *discipline*.

Intimacy is the state of being intimate, belonging to or characterizing one's deepest nature. Intimacy is marked by a very close association, contact, or familiarity. Relationally, intimacy is a warm and satisfying friendship developing through long association on a very personal and private level.

Cynthia and I met in the region of East Houston, near that ship channel area of southeast Texas. We dated and got to know each other better. We grew closer as we dated. Soon we became engaged. Eighteen months later, we married. After we married, we grew to know each other even more intimately. Now, after nearly fifty years of marriage, we have the most intimate of earthly relationships. Ours is a warm and satisfying, ever-developing closeness.

As I was preparing to preach on marriage at the Dallas Theological Seminary chapel, I came to the twenty-fifth verse in Genesis 2: "And the man and his wife were both naked and were not ashamed." The thought hit me: *That's the best description of intimacy.* It includes being emotionally naked and unashamed. You can be physically naked and unashamed with your partner in marriage. You can be so personally unguarded, you're able to share your deepest fear, your most guarded secret, or your most frightening thought, and you have no shame. That's intimacy.

But the ultimate is not an intimacy with one's partner in life; it is intimacy with the living God. Paul says, in effect, "My determined purpose is to be inwardly naked yet unashamed before Him, understanding the wonders of His person and the mystery of His will." Such divine intimacy is rare.

How distant are you from God right now? Has your closeness with Him chilled? Could that be why your worship has become so perfunctory? Do you sing the songs while thinking about something else? Are you so critical of your brothers and sisters in God's family that you sound just like an unbeliever, even though you know your place after death will be with God in heaven?

But the ultimate is not an intimacy with one's partner in life; it is intimacy with the living God.

Paul would respond this way: "My determined purpose is for that never to be true of me. I will pursue a relationship with Him that becomes so close, He and I will walk consistently together through whatever pressures that occur." That's intimacy. That's our goal.

Now, for the second word: *discipline*. This is the means for having intimacy with God.

Discipline is training that corrects and perfects our mental faculties or molds our moral character. Discipline is control gained by enforced obedience. It is the deliberate cultivation of inner order.

So how are intimacy and discipline connected? Let me repeat, if intimacy is the goal, discipline is the means to that end. Remember, intimacy is never natural, automatic, quick, or easy. Show me someone who is intimate with God, and I'll show you someone who can be compared to a beautiful garden without weeds. Because all gardens grow weeds, you can bet that someone has taken time to cultivate the good plants while rooting out the bad ones. People who are close to God cultivate a personal intimacy with Him like a good gardener cultivates beautiful flowers.

So intimacy is both a discipline and a goal—much like humility and prayer and sacrifice, and any of the other disciplines. Our great tendency in this age is to increase our speed, to run faster, even in the Christian life. In the process our walk with God stays shallow, and our tank runs low on fumes. Intimacy offers a full tank of fuel that can only be found by pulling up closer to God, which requires taking necessary time and going to the effort to make that happen. Remember, Paul said that his "determined purpose" (the discipline) was that he might "know God more intimately and personally" (the goal). Intimacy and discipline work together—and in the process, in a very real way, the means (discipline) leads to the very satisfying end (intimacy).

Discipline is the key.

After spending many months thinking about this, I have arrived at eight essential disciplines that lead to godliness:

1. Intimacy: Deepening Our Lives

2. Simplicity: Uncluttering Our Minds

3. Silence and Solitude: Slowing Our Pace

4. Surrender: Releasing Our Grip

5. Prayer: Calling Out

6. Humility: Bowing Low

7. Self-Control: Holding Back

8. Sacrifice: Giving Over

Notice that the first four disciplines have to do with getting rid of something, creating room in your life. The next four contribute vitality and authenticity to your spiritual life. We've already seen the value of the first essential.

Of course there are many other disciplines we could consider. And we could credibly argue for a shorter or longer list. I don't claim to have the definitive path to intimacy with the Almighty. But I can say that after forty years of ministry, having prescribed these to others and having applied them to my own life, these eight disciplines fall into the category of essentials.

Cultivate these disciplines, and your relationship with the Lord will flourish. More significantly, these will become paths that will lead you to becoming more like Christ.

Cultivate these disciplines, and your relationship with the Lord will flourish.

two

Simplicity:

Uncluttering Our Minds

One ship drives east and another drives west
With the selfsame winds that blow.
'Tis the set of the sails
And not the gales
Which tells us the way to go.
Like the winds of the sea are the ways of fate,
As we voyage along through life:
'Tis the set of a soul
That decides its goal,
And not the calm or the strife.

—ELLA WHEELER WILCOX

Simplicity:

Uncluttering Our Minds

Anyone who loves spending time near the surf or a lake has seen this scene take place. A prevailing wind may blow hard from the south, for example, yet boats on the water travel east or west. A seasoned sailor can even travel south, directly into that wind, using a technique called tacking. Though he cannot control the winds, the skipper knows how to sail. He swings the boom to orient his mainsail to catch the wind, then he turns his rudder to steer the craft virtually any direction he wishes.

Like the poet, my concern has little to do with sailing and everything to do with life. I've seen the gales of hardship sink one person while pushing another toward greatness. Joni Eareckson Tada comes to mind. This lovely and very capable woman was tragically left a quadriplegic after a diving accident. Nevertheless she turned her disability into an opportunity to challenge others to rise above and beyond mediocrity despite hardship. Meanwhile a brother or sister in Christ with the same physical limitations may drown in self-pity. The same circumstance that emotionally cripples one person strengthens the resolve of another, lays one believer low while lifting his brother to incredible heights. Interesting, isn't it? "'Tis the set of the sails, and not the gales, which tells us the way to go."

We all face similar obstacles to developing a deeper spiritual life—yet some maintain the status quo, while others greatly succeed. As we begin the journey toward an intimate, personal relationship with the Almighty Creator, let me offer a warning. Developing these disciplines into enduring habits will not come naturally, easily, automatically, or quickly. Don't let excuses justify quitting, and give yourself ample time. Remember that our desire is intimacy with God. Such intimacy grows into godliness. Not godliness on a schedule, but a growing Christlikeness that takes root in your soul and gradually takes over your whole self. That takes time. You're not going to become a Martin Luther by the weekend or a Mother Teresa by the end of the month.

The disciplines have given you the ability to choose your destination: intimacy with God that results in Christlikeness.

You will find that your mind needs time and experience in order to assimilate these concepts. They are foreign—very unnatural—to the natural mind. The natural state of mind for all of us is to satisfy physical wants—mostly legitimate ones—as a primary motivation in virtually every area of life. The disciplines are spiritual activities that feel awkward at first. Like any new model of behavior, they must be wrestled with, talked through, come to terms with, tried on. As time passes, and by the grace of God, a few of them will begin to settle into a routine. You will discover, looking back over a few months, that you have changed. How did it happen? You set your sails in a new direction, and you are no longer helplessly blown by the gusts of each gale. The disciplines have given you the ability to choose your destination: intimacy with God that results in Christlikeness. The simplicity of your choice helps unclutter your mind.

Remember our key verse? Here it is, again:

[For my determined purpose is] that I may know Him—that I may progressively become more deeply and intimately acquainted with Him, perceiving and recognizing and understanding [the wonders of His Person] more strongly and more clearly, and that I may in that same way come to know the power outflowing from His resurrection [which it exerts over believers]; and that I may so share His sufferings as to be continually transformed [in spirit into His likeness even] to His death.

—PHILIPPIANS 3:10 AMP

Notice the words "continually transformed." This perspective may also prove helpful: Christlikeness is a journey, not a destination—at least on this side of God's radical transformation of the world during the end times. The joy is in the journey. Plan on a lifetime of travel. While you're at it, learn to enjoy the ride, despite the inevitable wrong turns and sometime toilsome progress. The satisfaction and peace you gain far outweigh the inconvenience.

SOURCES OF MIND-CLUTTER

In order for intimacy with the Almighty to become our determined purpose, we will have to make some major changes. That process begins with an honest assessment of what stands in our way. The first and most obvious challenges we face are the enormous complications of this century and the resulting clutter it produces in our minds.

I can name at least five sources of mind-clutter common to the twenty-first century.

First, *most of us today say yes to far too many things.* That means we are busier than we need to be, perhaps because we fear the void in our souls that a few quiet hours might reveal. According to those he mentored, Lewis Sperry Chafer, founder of Dallas Theological Seminary, used to say, "Much of our activity today is little more than a cheap anesthetic to deaden the pain of an empty life."

Second, *most of us do not plan time for leisure and rejuvenation.* We dutifully pull out our day planner to fill the spaces between activities. But let's not kid ourselves; avoiding overlapping activities isn't planning. As a result, we're a hassled, short-tempered, horn-blowing society perpetually commuting between poorly planned activities that add very little to our well-being. Stop and think: when was the last time you marked off a block of time in your planner and wrote "rest" in the middle of it?

Third, *most of us rarely experience the joy of accomplishment.* A wise man once wrote, "A desire accomplished is sweet to the soul" (Proverbs 13:19 NKJV). But with too much to do, we dash off to the next obligation, often without finishing the previous one or taking the time to stand back and savor a job well done. No wonder so many worry that their existence seems meaningless. They're too hurried to feel the satisfaction they worked so hard—and fast—to earn.

Fourth, *most people living in wealthy countries owe more than they can hope to repay.* And to make matters worse, most are working their way even deeper into debt. Banks just keep handing out shiny plastic cards and finding more creative ways to thank us for handing over ever-increasing interest money. Another proverb says, "The borrower becomes the lender's slave" (Proverbs 22:7). Those cards hold us in bondage, resulting in plastic slavery—shackles that are brilliantly disguised as gold or platinum plastic cards with a magnetic strip. And the result? We can never fully enjoy what we have because the voice of our creditors continually whispers the reminder that we don't really own any of it.

Don't misunderstand. Credit cards can be a valuable money-management tool in the hands of a disciplined person. There is nothing inherently wrong with keeping one handy to regulate cash flow or to travel more safely and conveniently. However, people tend to use credit to cover important, yet not essential expenses when cash is short. Have you ever paused and considered that by whipping out that card, you may be denying God the opportunity to meet that need in His own way? Or perhaps the opportunity to show you how nonessential that expense really was? Next time you're faced with a credit-purchase decision, wait. Don't say no necessarily. Just wait. I challenge you to present your need to the Lord before presenting it to a bank, and see what He does with it.

Fifth, *most of us fool ourselves into thinking that with our modern technology, we have simplified our lives.* Truth be told, we have complicated them. I sincerely believe that technology is a gift from God, a part of what theologians often call "common grace"—undeserved favor commonly bestowed upon all humankind for no other reason than His great love for us. I admit that I have little use for the latest gadgets in my own day-to-day life, but I thank God for anything that makes a task easier or more efficient. But in an age when, thanks to technology, most everything requires a tiny fraction of the time it did just a century ago, we have less unoccupied time than ever! Rather than lighten our load, we've added more weight.

My sister, Luci, illustrates this absurdity with a humorous story. It seems that a harried traveler at an airport was worried about missing his plane. He had forgotten his wristwatch and couldn't locate a clock, so he ran up to a stranger who happened to be carrying a couple of large bags in his hands. He stopped the guy and asked, "Would you tell me what time it is?"

The fellow said, "Sure." He put both bags down, pulled up the sleeve on his wrist, and said, "It is exactly 5:09, the temperature outside is 73 degrees, and it is supposed to rain tonight. In London the sky is clear with a high today of 28 degrees Celsius, with the barometer at 29.14 and falling. Let's see, in Singapore the sun is shining brightly. And . . . oh, this is interesting. The moon will be full in Los Angeles tonight."

"Your watch tells you all of that?" said the traveler, with wonder.

"Sure. In fact, it tells me much more. You see, I invented this watch, and I can assure you there's no other timepiece on earth like it."

"That's a watch I simply must have!" exclaimed the traveler. "May I buy it? I'll give you two thousand dollars for it. I've got the cash right here."

"No," replied the inventor, "it's not for sale." Then he reached down to pick up his suitcases and started to leave.

"Wait!" the first man insisted. "How about three thousand dollars?"

The inventor paused, shook his head, and said, "No. You see, I can't sell it to you. I made this watch for my son. I invented it for him to enjoy."

"Okay, five thousand dollars. I will give you five thousand dollars cash."

"No. I'm sorry. It's not for sale."

By now the traveler had grown desperate. "Ten thousand dollars! I want that watch."

The inventor couldn't believe his ears. "Ten thousand dollars? You'll give me ten thousand dollars for this watch?"

And the traveler said, "I will. I've got the money."

"Okay," said the inventor, "it's a deal," and he held out his hand for the money. After counting out the ten thousand dollars, the traveler grabbed the watch as soon as the inventor could take it off. A great satisfied smile stretched across his face as he snapped the wristwatch on and started to walk away. But before he could take a step, the inventor stopped him. "Wait!" As he reached down for the bags, he said, "Don't forget the batteries."

We hope the latest high-tech gadgetry will be the very thing that will set our schedule free. But in the end it weighs us down; it increases our dependency on something that will eventually break or become obsolete next week with the next marvel of modern science.

It's time we counted the hidden cost before investing more money and more confidence in the next does-it-all watch. Those batteries get awfully heavy once the novelty has worn off.

SIMPLIFY, SIMPLIFY

Aleksandr Solzhenitsyn once wrote:

> Do not pursue what is illusory. All that is gained at the expense of your nerves decade after decade and is confiscated in the fell of night. Live with the steady superiority over life. Don't be afraid of misfortune. Do not yearn after happiness. It is, after all, all the same. The bitter doesn't last forever. And the sweet never fills the cup to overflowing. It is enough if you don't freeze in the cold. And if thirst and hunger don't claw at your insides, if your back isn't broken, if your feet can walk and your arms can bend, if both eyes can see, if both ears hear, then whom . . . whom should you envy?[1]

The words of Henry Thoreau haunt me on occasion: "Our life is frittered away by detail. Simplify. Simplify."[2] There's a lot of frustration in the words "frittered away," isn't there? Matter of fact, you may have to admit that your life is frittered away by detail.

Paul the apostle was probably among the most fearless men in the Bible, yet he admitted a major fear. He shared his concern in a letter he wrote to the church in Corinth:

> For I am jealous for you with a godly jealousy; for I betrothed you to one husband, so that to Christ I might present you as a pure virgin. But I am afraid that, as the serpent deceived Eve by his craftiness, your minds will be led astray from the simplicity and purity of devotion to Christ. For if one comes and preaches another Jesus whom we have not preached, or you receive a different spirit which you have not received, or a different gospel which you have not accepted, you bear this beautifully.
>
> —2 CORINTHIANS 11:2–4

Take note of his concern: that their "minds will be led astray." From what? Simplicity. Purity.

A groom wants little more than the assurance of beginning an intimate life with a virgin bride. And no groom would tolerate a rival as the couple approaches the day of marriage—nor should he. With this same kind of protectiveness, Paul said, "I'm jealous for you." By way of illustration he likened himself to a matchmaker having promised a pure bride to her groom, and the apostle wanted nothing more than for his Master to be pleased.

Furthermore he said, "I am afraid." Afraid of what? "That, as the serpent deceived Eve by his craftiness, your minds will be led astray from the simplicity and purity of devotion to Christ" (v. 3). The Greek word Paul used is *exapataō,* which carries the dual meaning: deceive or entice. Put these two English words together and you get *seduction.* I like Eugene Peterson's paraphrase:

And now I'm afraid that exactly as the Snake seduced Eve with his smooth patter, you are being lured away from the simple purity of your love for Christ.

—2 CORINTHIANS 11:3 MSG

Read that again slowly. Pause to ponder the words "seduced" and "lured away." Both are like erosion, silent and slow and subtle. But talk about damaging!

The apostle started with the illustration of a bride and groom, and he went all the way back to the account in Genesis 3, where the serpent presented himself to the first woman and used his beauty to win her interest. He wooed her and convinced her that eating the fruit that God had forbidden would be good for her and her husband. He seduced her into believing a lie. He did it by craftiness. "My fear," Paul said, "is that your mind, like hers, will be led astray from a devoted, love relationship with your Husband—your Groom—Christ."

Notice that we're not left to wonder what made him so afraid. Verse 4 begins with "For," which signals that the next sentence will validate his fear: a pattern in their behavior that demonstrated the high likelihood that someone might seduce them, entice them to stray:

For if one comes and preaches another Jesus whom we have not preached, or you receive a different spirit which you have not received, or a different gospel which you have not accepted, you bear this beautifully.

—2 CORINTHIANS 11:4

Alfred Plummer, a fine New Testament commentator, pointed out that the apostle's fear was that the community would be seduced by the promise of increased knowledge. "Like the serpent, the false teachers were promising enlightenment as a reward of disloyalty and disobedience."[3] Sounds a lot like what seduced Eve in Genesis 3, doesn't it?

THE VIRTUE OF SIMPLICITY

In many ways, we're seeing that today. Many seducers clutter the simple message of the gospel with legalistic additions, with convoluted attempts to legitimize moral compromise, and with psychological theories that turn churches into relational support groups instead of houses of worship. The message of Christianity is quickly becoming a system of enlightened thinking instead of a simple call to turn from sin and pursue a relationship with God. The desire for greater theological knowledge (as good as that is) has supplanted the simple call to know Him intimately . . . in the power of His resurrection and in sharing His suffering. The simple message that Jesus proclaimed doesn't require a giant theological intellect in order to receive it and implement it. If generations of illiterate peasants throughout the centuries before us could do it, so can we—as long as we aren't seduced by the contemporary "enlightenment" surrounding us, enticing us to abandon what God has made simple.

The desire for greater theological knowledge . . . has supplanted the simple call to know Him intimately.

Notice the seduction Paul feared for the Corinthian believers: "But I am afraid that, as the serpent deceived Eve by his craftiness, your minds will be led astray *from the simplicity and purity of devotion to Christ*" (2 Corinthians 11:3, emphasis added).

Again, I urge you to focus fully on simplicity, on purity.

Alan Redpath, in a fine book titled *Blessings Out of Buffetings,* writes of the simplicity in Christ:

That is an arresting phrase because in these days there is scarcely anything that is simple; everything is so complicated. What I am I to believe? What is right? What is wrong? In every area of life the old simplicities have vanished from us until even this word *simple* has changed, and I don't think people like being called *simple* anymore because it has an association that is unpleasant![4]

Think about that. Would you like someone to say of you, "Well, she's a simple woman," or "He's a simple man"? *Simple* used to be a compliment, meaning unwavering, disciplined, determined, moving in a clearly defined direction—but not now. Now it suggests you're not operating at full capacity above the shoulders! Your elevator doesn't reach the top floor. Both oars aren't in the water.

The New Testament word, however, calls to mind a piece of cloth without a crease in it. When describing people, the Greek term *haplotēs* means "singleness."

Redpath continues:

All the great men of God have been so simple, just as little children. I could bring in an array of them (I wish I could in person) to your mind—Isaiah and Paul from the Word of God, Bunyan, William Carey, Handley Moule, Hudson Taylor, D. L. Moody, Adoniram Judson, to mention just a few, but these men with brilliant minds were basically as simple as little children in their walk with God. A man may be a saint without having many of the qualities which the world today rates very highly, but he will never be a saint without simplicity of soul, a simplicity that is in Christ. It was this that burned in the heart of Martin Luther in the days of the Reformation when he said, "Let us get through to God. Give us a basic, dynamic, personal simplicity of faith in Jesus Christ."[5]

CLUTTER AS THE ENEMY OF SIMPLICITY

Paul feared that a rival gospel, promising enlightenment, would woo the congregation of Corinth away from their faith in Christ. And he had good reason to fear such spiritual erosion. Because they failed to maintain a single-eyed devotion to Christ, they were a pliable bunch, susceptible to distraction and given to extremes.

I fear the same for us. I'm not worried that a false gospel will carry us away but that our simple devotion to Christ will be lost among the clutter. That we'll be consumed by complication—trivial distractions that swirl around in our minds and blow us randomly about so that at the end of our lives, we may as well have pursued heresy.

> One ship drives east and another drives west
> With the selfsame winds that blow.
> 'Tis the set of the sails
> And not the gales
> Which tells us the way to go.

Where is your ship going? Is it blown here and there by the shifting winds of complication? Is anyone at the helm? Are you reacting to the needs of the immediate or ordering your priorities to enjoy deeper devotion to Jesus Christ? Have you found yourself working harder, not for the satisfaction of a job well done but to keep one step ahead of your creditors? Do you use technology to simplify your life, or do you spend much of your time and money maintaining your gadgets?

Before rushing on, force yourself to answer those searching questions.

Too much clutter in your mind leaves insufficient room for devotion to Christ. And it shows up in how you relate to Him. For instance, do you take time to pray? I don't mean hours of prayer. I don't believe that's practical or even wise. I read of some saints who saved four hours out of the middle of the day for prayer, and I wondered, *How did they earn a living? Who had to sacrifice his or her own prayer time to supplement those extra hours needed to support that praying saint?* So I'm not even suggesting four hours. How about only four minutes a day?

*T*oo much clutter in your mind leaves insufficient room for devotion to Christ.

What about meditation? Not Eastern meditation, where you empty your mind of all thought; I mean biblical meditation. Psalm 1 meditation: "You thrill to GOD's Word, you chew on Scripture day and night" (Psalm 1:2 MSG). Like a cow chewing the cud, you turn over a thought or a passage of God's Word in your mind and chew on it until it makes sense. Just try to do that with a cluttered, stressed-out mind.

I read the thoughts of long-gone saints in books, now out of print—those great, old, leather-bound volumes in my library. Those long-ago authors took a lot of time to turn over a phrase in their mind. They held it up to the light to examine it from one angle, then got underneath it to look at it from that perspective, and then held it against the mirror of Scripture. They were meditating with ink on paper, and the result is marvelous! They didn't write to entertain the hurried reader. They couldn't have cared less if their book was marketed or if it sold a hundred copies. They didn't write to make a best-seller list; they wrote in order to deepen. And you can tell it! They poured their thoughts on paper, assuming the reader would also take time to turn it over in his or her mind.

Now relax . . . you don't need a library full of leather-bound volumes in order to meditate. But you do need to invest the time and the energy to cultivate a depth of devotion. It is *that* which requires us to simplify—to unclutter our lives, to weed the garden of our minds to make room for something beautiful to grow.

Let me probe even deeper. How are things in the pride department? Perhaps you do devote sufficient time to prayer and meditation, but maybe you've begun to get a little sophisticated—or, as we say in Texas, a little uppity! You may have taken some courses at a Bible school or benefited by the teaching of a strong and faithful minister of the gospel. It's possible you may have even earned an advanced degree in theology. Wonderful! But has that complicated your simple devotion? Maybe the serpent has seduced you with a desire to appear a little more intellectual, a little less emotional, a little more aloof and stiff.

I'll never forget a letter I read from a graduate of Dallas Theological Seminary, where I serve as chancellor. He wrote of his gratitude for his years at our fine institution. What troubled me was that he also lamented that when he arrived, he was deeply in love with Jesus Christ; but when he left, he had fallen more in love with the biblical text. For all the right reasons, our professors did their best to teach him the Scriptures, but he left loving the Bible more than he loved His Savior. To use Paul's words, "the serpent seduced him." After a few tough years in ministry, he came to realize that he needed to love *Christ*. I don't remember his using these precise words, but he admitted that he had to look intently at his schedule, to face the truth of his drift, and to carve out time to get back to a simple devotion to Christ.

The point of the passage is clear and the principle is straightforward. So what's left is the importance of application. What are specific ways we should incorporate this new understanding so that we become more like Jesus Christ? As we turn our attention from hearing to doing, I want to address both your private life and your public (or relational) life.

MAINTAINING AN UNCLUTTERED PRIVATE LIFE

First, think of your own personal life. Someday you will lie in a casket as your loved ones weep over your departure and then place you in the ground. On that day you will stand on your own before God to give an account of the deeds done during your earthly life (see 2 Corinthians 5:9–10). It's just you and your Lord.

Forget about your loved ones, your friends, and most especially that person you think needs this book more than you do. Think only about yourself right now. As you do, consider two questions:

First, *do you spend adequate time with God?* I mean private time all alone with Him. Would you find it helpful to begin simplifying your schedule so that you can begin meeting with God, even if it is for fifteen minutes each day? Fifteen uninterrupted minutes . . . away from people, with the television and the radio turned off. Time spent alone in the backyard or a local park or even in your car, if that's the only place you can find to be alone. What about your lunch hour on a bench somewhere away from the office? Does your office have a door you can close?

I have to admit that, even as a pastor, setting aside time to be alone and silent before Him is one of the toughest priorities I have to maintain. You would think that would be easy for someone whose vocation is spiritual leadership, but, believe me, the temptation to be busy is as powerful in ministry as anywhere. There's always a good reason to leave the Master's feet to do His work—or so we convince ourselves. So, to protect that time, I've had to make one tiny yet powerful word a regular part of my vocabulary.

The word is *no.*

We can make our lives as complicated or as simple as we desire with a kind, polite, respectful, yet all-important *no.*

And perhaps it's time to back out of a few things to which we said yes. You can be sure there will be consequences. Some may think less of you or see you as a quitter. Even so, keep your eye on the goal, prepare to be misunderstood, respond with patience, but remain firm. Your no to others will soon translate into a yes for God.

This may be especially difficult for you if you are multitalented. Chances are good that a person with a limited number of abilities has

Y*our no to others will soon translate into a yes for God.*

a less complicated life than those of you who are good at several things. You can speak, you can sing, you can organize, you can put meetings together, you get things done, and you're disciplined in those areas; so people naturally call on you. I read years ago that the world is run by tired people. I think that's true. You've heard the adage, "If you want to get something done, ask somebody who's busy." Well, maybe it's time for you, the busy person, to say, "No, not this year. I won't be the one in charge of the picnic." Or, "No, I'm not able to plan the pre-Easter service." Or, "I'm sorry, I can't do what I thought I could when I said yes earlier. Please find someone else."

Just say no.

Second, *have you become a cluttered person within?* Our surroundings often reflect what's going on inside. When my desk, my closet, and my car start getting cluttered, that's a signal that my life has accumulated needless extras while I wasn't paying attention. It's normal. That can happen to anyone who is productive. But it can't stay that way.

Look around you. Go ahead and do that right now. Look in your closet. The next time you walk into your office, take an objective look at your desk. Open the trunk of your car. What does it look like? Some reading this have to rake stuff out of the passenger seat before giving their friend a ride. What if we took a quick look inside your briefcase? How about your garage? If you are like most people, your mind is just as cluttered. No room, no quiet space, no time for God. A life so littered with the trivial that simple devotion to your Maker feels like a wistful luxury you can never afford. If so, it's time for some spring-cleaning.

MAINTAINING AN UNCLUTTERED PUBLIC LIFE

Now let's think about your public life: your world of relationships, your social involvements and activities with other people. Take a few moments in quiet to answer these questions.

Are good things keeping you from choosing God's best? The process of simplifying life can be a very painful process involving some extremely difficult decisions.

Remember our key verse for this book? "[For my determined purpose is] that I may know Him—that I may progressively become more deeply and intimately acquainted with Him" (Philippians 3:10 AMP). Look at what Paul said just a few verses later about how he was trying to accomplish that goal. "I do not regard myself as having laid hold of it yet; but one thing I do: forgetting what lies behind and reaching forward to what lies ahead, I press on toward the goal for the prize of the upward call of God in Christ Jesus" (Philippians 3:13–14).

Cynthia and I recently came to a place that required just such a decision. For twenty years we hosted the annual Insight for Living family conference at Mount Hermon in Northern California. I cannot tell you how many wonderful memories we have of that place. Our children grew up with that event as a regular part of their lives. It became a significant part of the Swindoll family heritage. Our broadcast ministry enjoyed connecting with a large number of our listeners year after year, but we finally had to realize how much time and energy and money it required for us to continue hosting that conference.

We finally had to calculate the enormous resources that it takes to host this conference as we mapped the future direction of Insight for Living. We felt certain that God would have us focus our attention more specifically in one area of need virtually untouched by other ministries. To continue the Mount Hermon tradition merely for the sake of meeting with friends would limit how effective we could be. At that time, to return to Mount Hermon would have been holding on to something very, very good but forfeiting God's best for us as a ministry.

Doing anything, just because you've always done it, is a classic example of clutter.

Look at the example Jesus gave us. When He came to the end of His earthly ministry, though only thirty-three years old, He said boldly, "I glorified You on the earth, having accomplished the work which You have given Me to do" (John 17:4). That's an uncluttered life. He could have gotten much more involved with the twelve disciples, or He could have chosen twenty-five disciples to more than double His earthly outreach. He could have traveled to Rome, the seat of civilization at the time, or to Athens, where He could touch great minds in order to extend the impact of His ministry to a much broader base of humanity.

But Jesus chose only twelve disciples. He mentored them slowly and intimately and never traveled very far from the place of His birth. Some might say that if you're going to revolutionize the world, you need to carry your cause to as many parts of it as possible. But Jesus deliberately limited His itinerary. He kept His ministry simple. At the end, just before breathing His last, He said, "It is finished."

I admit to reading perhaps too much into those words, but I see contentment there. Jesus was ready to die because there was nothing left for Him to do on earth. All the work had been completed, from the training of disciples to providing redemption for humanity. I detect no hint of resignation or regret in any of His last words. Mission accomplished.

Are too many material possessions draining your energy, leaving you exhausted and maybe even resentful? Simplifying may call for unloading some of your material possessions that require so much of your time, energy, and money that you should invest elsewhere. Consider selling or perhaps giving away some of those burdens.

Cynthia and I needed less than seventy-two hours to decide that the Swindoll family had no need for an RV. For many years, camping had been a fun way for us to enjoy time together, so we thought we'd take it a step further as we bought this behemoth of a vehicle. I think it came with its own zip code. The steering wheel looked like it had been pulled out of a Greyhound bus, and twelve car batteries ran the electrical system, which the refrigerator drained in one night. Try finding a place that will recharge a dozen DieHard batteries out in the middle of nowhere!

By the time we drove this monster from the factory in Oregon to Southern California, we realized that this vehicle was going own *us*. We hadn't even reached home before we said to each other, "We're going to drive ourselves crazy trying to maintain this thing." Rather than allow something to consume valuable resources, we chose to simplify. We chose to eliminate something nice but unnecessary in favor of other things that would deepen our marriage, enhance our family, and strengthen our relationship with Jesus Christ.

Are activities outside your home stealing time from those within the home? Project yourself several years into the future for a glimpse of your children as adults. How old will your children be in twenty or thirty years? How will they remember you? Will they have memories of you other than your leaving for and returning from work and other important activities?

I suspect that if you are like most men and women living in developed countries, you have convinced yourself that the best way you can serve your family is to nurture a career that will ensure a stable, sizable income; one that will provide security and comfort. Or you may be gratified by a long list of activities, each one good in its own right but keeping you out more evenings than in.

Consider this excerpt from *On the Road with Charles Kuralt*. I remember seeing the correspondent capture this scene on camera. I also remember marveling at the simplicity of the scene and of the people in it.

A long road took nine children out of the cotton fields, out of poverty, out of Mississippi. But the roads go both ways, and this Thanksgiving weekend, they all returned. This is about Thanksgiving, and coming home.

One after another, and from every corner of America, the cars turned into the yard. With much cheering and much hugging, the nine children of Alex and Mary Chandler were coming home for their parents' fiftieth wedding anniversary.

Gloria Chandler: There's my daddy. *[Gloria rushes to hug him.]*

Gloria Chandler Coleman, master of arts, University of Missouri, a teacher in Kansas City, was home.

All nine children had memories of a sharecropper's cabin and nothing to wear and nothing to eat. All nine are college graduates.

Cooking the meal in the kitchen of the new house the children built for their parents four years ago is Bessie Chandler Beasley, BA Tuskegee, MA Central Michigan, dietitian at a veterans hospital, married to a Ph.D. And helping out, Princess Chandler Norman, MA Indiana University, a school teacher in Gary, Indiana. You'll meet them all.

But first, I thought you ought to meet their parents. Alex Chandler remembers the time when he had a horse and a cow and tried to buy a mule and couldn't make the payments and lost the mule, the horse, and the cow. And about that time, Cleveland, the first son, decided he wanted to go to college.

Alex Chandler: We didn't have any money. And we went to town; he wanted to catch the bus to go on up there. And so we went to town and borrowed two dollars and a half from her niece, and bought him a bus ticket. And when he got there, that's all he had.

From that beginning, he became Dr. Cleveland Chandler. He is chairman of the economics department at Howard University. How did they do it, starting on one of the poorest farms in the poorest part of the poorest state in America?

Princess Chandler Norman: We worked.

Kuralt: You picked cotton?

Norman: Yes, picked cotton, and pulled corn, stripped millet, dug potatoes.

They all left. Luther left for the University of Omaha and went on to become the Public Service Employment Manager for Kansas City. He helped his younger brother, James, come to Omaha University, too, and go on to graduate work at Yale. And in his turn, James helped Herman, who graduated from Morgan State and is a technical manager in Dallas. And they helped themselves. Fortson, a Baptist Minister in Pueblo, Colorado, wanted to go to Morehouse College.

Fortson Chandler: I chose Morehouse and it was difficult. I had to pick cotton all summer long to get the first month's rent and tuition.

So, helping themselves and helping one another, they all went away. And now, fifty years after life began for the Chandler family in a one-room shack in a cotton field, now, just as they were sitting down in the new house to the ham and turkey and sweet potatoes and cornbread and collard greens and two kinds of pie and three kinds of cake, now Donald arrived—the youngest—who had driven with his family all the way down from Minneapolis. And now the Chandlers were all together again.

Alex Chandler *[saying grace]:* Our Father in heaven, we come at this moment, giving thee thanks for thou hast been so good and so kind. We want to thank you, oh God, for this, for your love and for your Son. Thank you that you have provided for all of us through all these years. *[Mr. Chandler begins weeping.]*

Remembering all those years of sharecropping and going hungry and working for a white man for fifty cents a day and worrying about his children's future, remembering all that, Alex Chandler almost didn't get through this blessing.

Alex *[continuing grace]:* In Jesus's name, amen.

And neither did the others. *[Family members wiping tears away]*

The Chandler family started with as near nothing as any family in America ever did. And so their Thanksgiving weekend might have more thankful than most. *[Chandler family singing "I'll Fly Away."]*

"I'll Fly Away" is the name of an old hymn. It is Mr. Chandler's favorite. His nine children flew away, and made places for themselves in this country; and this weekend, came home again.

There probably are no lessons in any of this, but I know that in the future whenever I hear that the family is a dying institution, I'll think of them. Whenever I hear anything in America is impossible, I'll think of them.[6]

The Chandler children are a testament to the power of their parents' influence despite the lack of a stable, secure income. Their simplicity, though forced by harsh economic realities, yielded strong, resilient men and women of amazing character and an unshakable faith in God.

I would never suggest that anyone should choose poverty—especially one that stark—for the sake of simplicity. But I can say with confidence that we'll be no less rich having given up a few unnecessary commitments to be at home.

SIMPLICITY LEADS TO INTIMACY

When you first thought about the spiritual disciplines, what was your first emotion? Be honest. Did you groan just a little? Did the thought of adding another duty, another activity feel burdensome? *How can I possibly give more _____ (you fill in the blank) to God when I'm already running in the red?*

> One ship drives east and another drives west
> With the selfsame winds that blow.
> 'Tis the set of the sails
> And not the gales
> Which tells us the way to go.

Are you going where you want to go, or are the gales of a complicated life pushing you away from the best destination? Simplify. Your journey toward intimacy includes the discipline of simplicity, which, by its exercise, leaves you with more time, not less. And because this discipline is an exercise in subtraction, the fruit of it is additional room—margin, some call it—to enjoy a long-lasting, satisfying, rewarding, *intimate* relationship with God.

three

Silence and Solitude:

Slowing Our Pace

May not the inadequacy of much of our spiritual experience be traced back to our habit of skipping through the corridors of the Kingdom like children in the market place, chattering about everything, but pausing to learn the value of nothing.[1]

—A. W. TOZER

Silence and Solitude:

Slowing Our Pace

Do you see anything?" The four-word question must have made both men smile as they reminisced later. It came from Lord Archie Canarvan as Dr. Howard Carter, the renowned British archaeologist, poked his head through an opening he had made into an ancient Egyptian tomb. After six challenging years of digging, Canarvan's funding and Carter's searching had yielded only a maze of trenches, tons of sand and rock, and mounds of worthless debris. Nothing! That is, until this most unusual, history-making day in November 1922.

You see, everyone else had dug into the Royal Valley and said there was nothing else to be discovered, nothing left to be found. This, of course, made the question all the more ironic as Dr. Carter stared in disbelief into this ancient tomb.

Peering into silent darkness, Dr. Carter saw wooden animals, statues, chests, gilded chariots, carved cobras, unguent boxes, vases, daggers, jewels, a throne, a wooden figure of the goddess Selket, and a hand-carved coffin of a teenage king. In his own words, he saw "strange animals, statues, and gods—everywhere the glint of gold."[2] It was, of course, the priceless tomb and treasures of King Tutankhamen, the world's most exciting archaeological discovery up to that time in history. There were more than three thousand objects in all, taking Dr. Carter the next ten years to remove, catalog, and restore.

"Exquisite!" "Incredible!" "Elegant!" "Magnificent!" These must have been the words uttered by Dr. Carter and his patron, who had earlier asked, "Do you see anything?"

The treasures unearthed from that magnificent Egyptian tomb, however, cannot compare to the riches—these left by a living King— that lay waiting to be found in God's Word. The inspired words of Proverbs 2:1–5 were given to Solomon to pass on to his son, words of wisdom that could make us rich:

> My son, if you will receive my words
> And treasure my commandments within you,
> Make your ear attentive to wisdom,
> Incline your heart to understanding;
> For if you cry for discernment,
> Lift your voice for understanding;
> If you seek her as silver
> And search for her as for hidden treasures;
> Then you will discern the fear of the LORD
> And discover the knowledge of God.

James Moffat, in his quaint translation of the Bible, renders that last verse: "Then you shall see what reverence for the Eternal is, and find out what the knowledge of God means" (Proverbs 2:5 MOFFAT).

Notice the number of conditions Solomon introduced by the small word "if":

"My son, if . . ." (v. 1)

"For if . . ." (v. 3)

"If . . ." (v. 4)

All of these conditions point to our responsibility. "If you will do this, child of God; if you will do that, woman of God, man of God; if you will pay the price, if you will go to the hard work of digging and digging and digging even more, then," verse 5 promises, "you will make some magnificent discoveries, then you will come to see what the knowledge of God means." I would paraphrase it: "Then you will understand what it means to know God."

Edwin Hodder wrote one of my favorite hymns back in 1914, "Thy Word Is Like a Garden." Unfortunately, you won't find it in any of our modern hymnals:

> Thy Word is like a deep, deep mine; and jewels rich and rare
> Are hidden in its mighty depths for every searcher there.[3]

In the pages of this book we're engaged in an excavation of our own, digging for secrets, searching for treasures that will deepen our intimacy with God. But if we are to search with integrity and diligence, we must be ready to see what others miss as we dig through the sand, rocks, and rubble of the familiar into places where many others would say, "There's nothing left to be found."

Church can be a lot like that. Bible study can be drier than the desert sands of Egypt when we forget what we're pursuing. So it shouldn't be surprising that many of us, after all our searching, would have to admit that we have not "progressively become more deeply and intimately acquainted with Him" (Philippians 3:10 AMP).

Deep within our souls we still long to know God intimately.

Sure, we've attended worship services, we've sung the songs, and we've even taken good notes in more Bible studies than we can number. But deep within our souls we still long to know God intimately. Oh, to be less surprised at His magnificent answers to prayer . . . to have more trust and less anxiety . . . to be genuinely Christian to the core of our beings . . . to be less religious and more like Christ! *What a treasure is Christlikeness!*

I am more convinced than ever that those longings are possible to satisfy. The journey toward deeper intimacy with the Almighty begins with a decision to reorder our lives according to a different set of priorities. And just like an archaeological dig, the process isn't easy. It's hard work, but I can guarantee that you will find it worth the effort.

CEASE!

Thanks to Martin Luther, Psalm 46 has come to be known as "The Battle Hymn of the Reformation." The opening words of this psalm inspired the German reformer to write his most famous hymn, *"Ein' feste Burg ist unser Gott."* We know it today as "A Mighty Fortress Is Our God."

I found these words from historian Philip Schaff fascinating:

To Luther belongs the extraordinary merit of having given to the German people in their own tongue, and in a form eclipsing and displacing all former versions, the Bible, the catechism, and the hymn-book, so that God might speak directly to them in His word, and that they might directly speak to Him in their songs. He was a musician also, and composed tunes to some of his hymns. He is the Ambrose of German church poetry and church music. He wrote thirty-seven hymns. Most of them (twenty-one) date from the year 1524; the first from 1523, soon after the completion of his translation of the New Testament; the last two from 1543, three years before his death. The most original and best known—we may say the most Luther-like and most Reformer-like—is that historic and battle- and victory-hymn of the Reformation, which has so often been reproduced in other languages, and resounds in all German lands with mighty effect on great occasions:—

"Ein' feste Burg ist unser Gott."

(A tower of strength is our God.)[4]

Even a casual reading of Psalm 46 reveals the theme: God is our refuge and strength.

"God is in the midst of her" (v. 5), meaning the city of Jerusalem.

"The LORD of hosts is with us" (v. 7).

"The LORD of hosts is with us, the God of Jacob is our stronghold" (v. 11).

The composer's repetition drives the point home: God is in control. God is in our midst. God is with us. God is our protection.

If you read through Psalm 46, you observe that the word *Selah* appears three times in the ancient song. According to Hebrew scholars, this most likely means "pause." A good friend of mine liked to translate *Selah* as "Pause, and let that sink in." Perhaps musicians singing this song would pause for listeners to consider carefully the profound words they had just heard.

This inspired *Selah* provides a built-in outline for the psalm. Each interlude punctuates a description of a life-threatening situation in which, despite the appearance of danger, God is still in control.

THE UPHEAVAL OF NATURE

Therefore we will not fear, though the earth should change,
And though the mountains slip into the heart of the sea;
Though its waters roar and foam,
Though the mountains quake at its swelling pride.

Selah.

—PSALM 46:2-3

Even if mountains, the most stable, predictable objects in nature, should suddenly collapse, the reaction of those whose hearts are fixed on God will not be fear. In the deepest part of their being, people with an intimate relationship with God know that He is still in control, "a very *present* help in trouble."

THE ASSAULT OF ENEMIES

There is a river whose streams make glad the city of God,
The holy dwelling places of the Most High.
God is in the midst of her, she will not be moved;
God will help her when morning dawns.
The nations made an uproar, the kingdoms tottered;

He raised His voice, the earth melted.
The LORD of hosts is with us; the God of Jacob is our stronghold.

Selah.

—PSALM 46:4–7

To those living in Palestine, throughout all of history up to this present day, Jerusalem is the prize city, the gem of all jewels, the center of their geographical lives. The heart of every true Jew beats for Jerusalem, as did the heart of this composer. Though besieged by great empires, God will protect her.

THE VIOLENCE OF WAR

Come, behold the works of the LORD,
Who has wrought desolations in the earth.
He makes wars to cease to the end of the earth;
He breaks the bow and cuts the spear in two;
He burns the chariots with fire.
"Cease striving and know that I am God;
I will be exalted among the nations, I will be exalted in the earth."
The LORD of hosts is with us;
The God of Jacob is our stronghold.

Selah.

—PSALM 46:8–11

One Hebrew term attracts me to this psalm: a very small imperative, a terse command. Preceded by images of chaos—mountains sliding into the ocean, cities under attack, breaking bows, and burning chariots—comes the absurd command, "Cease!" *Rāphah* is the Hebrew term. It could be rendered: Relax. Be quiet. Quit. Do nothing. When

59

danger threatens someone, we might naturally panic as we shout, "Run!" "Duck!" or "Get out!" But God says, "Cease." Imagine someone calling into a burning building, "Do nothing!"

According to Harris, Archer, and Waltke, in their well-respected work, *Theological Wordbook of the Old Testament*, "The Hiphil stem is the most common in usage with twenty-one occurrences. It usually means 'to let drop,' 'to abandon' in this form (Josh 10:6; Deut 4:31 et al). It also means to 'let alone,' 'refrain' (Jud 11:37; Ps 37:8)."[5]

Psalm 37:8 uses the command this way: "Cease from anger and forsake wrath; do not fret; it leads only to evildoing." In this verse the Hebrew verb points to an object. "Cease anger." But in Psalm 46 the command simply says, "Stop!" Your translation may supply the word "striving" for clarity, but the verb stands quietly alone in the original language. "Stop!" says it all. Think of a parent whose kids are out of control, crawling all over the backseat, throwing things at each other, and yelling and complaining. Finally Mom or Dad simply says, "Stop!" No need for details.

In the midst of danger and turmoil, God commands, "Cease!"

Eugene Peterson's paraphrase of the Scriptures, *The Message,* aptly captures the concept: "Step out of the traffic! Take a long, loving look at Me, your High God, above politics, above everything" (Psalm 46:10 MSG). The King James Version is probably the most familiar: "Be still, and know that I am God" (Psalm 46:10 KJV).

Most of us find this command extremely difficult to obey. Any who have tried to do so quickly discover a perplexing truth: we can't stop striving on our own. This has to start with God's convincing us of its value from within. Yet it's universal. The intended audience would include those outside Israel—the nations. This is a command to anyone who hears or reads the psalm. And it's not a casual suggestion; it's a strong command. This isn't a neat idea reserved for those rare occasions when things seem to be getting out of control; it's a call to a habitual, customary attitude of stillness before Almighty God.

"Be still."

JOURNEY INTO SILENCE

As we continue our journey toward intimacy with the Almighty, Psalm 46:10 calls us to the discipline of silence. Silence is the by-product of being still. What happens when you and I commit ourselves to periods of absolute, uninterrupted silence? Look back at the tenth verse. We discover who God is. "Cease, so that you might know that I am God."

How can silence yield such a revelation? Candidly I cannot fully explain it. I just know that somehow the Spirit of God reveals Himself when we shut out loud and busy distractions, close our mouths for a protracted period of time, and listen.

Former CBS anchor Dan Rather found himself unprepared for a television interview with Mother Teresa several years ago. Ron Mehl described the newsman's encounter this way:

Somehow, all of his standard approaches and formula questions were inadequate for the task, and the little nun from Calcutta, sitting beside him so sweetly and tranquilly, didn't seem inclined to make his task easier.

"When you pray," asked Rather, "what do you say to God?"

"I don't say anything," she replied. "I listen."

Rather tried another tack. "Well, okay . . . when God speaks to you, then, what does He say?"

"He doesn't say anything. He listens."

Rather looked bewildered. For an instant, he didn't know what to say.

"And if you don't understand that," Mother Teresa added, "I can't explain it to you."[6]

I loved that interview!

This is one of those mysteries with which I am content to confess my ignorance and encourage you to discover its secrets for yourself. As the Scottish say, "Some things are better felt than telt." You're on your own with this one. Perhaps this is why the Scriptures speak of "the mystery of godliness" (1 Timothy 3:16).

Remember the conditions of Proverbs 2? If we do our part in obedience to the command, God will be faithful to respond. If you will cease, then God will reveal. The opposite is also implied. If you refuse to be still, if you do not seek times for silence and solitude, you may gain some knowledge *about* God without knowing *Him* at all. It is through times of silence and protracted periods of stillness that He makes Himself real.

Look at what Paul had to say about this mystery. In describing what it means for a believer to live in the Spirit, he said, "The Spirit himself bears witness to our spirit that we are God's children" (Romans 8:16 NET). Eugene Peterson's paraphrased translation captures the full meaning of this: "God's Spirit touches our spirits and confirms who we really are. We know who he is, and we know who we are: Father and children" (Romans 8:16 MSG).

Looking back at another bit of Solomon's wisdom, written for his son and preserved for us, I find, "Watch over your heart with all diligence, for from it flow the springs of life" (Proverbs 4:23).

Speaking of the heart, Solomon counsels, "Guard it." Based on my study of this verse in Hebrew, given its context and taking into account the nuances of the terms Solomon used, I would paraphrase it this way: "Above all else to be closely watched and protected, it is imperative that you preserve and keep sensitive your heart, because from within it come the decisions and characteristics that define your life."

Let me suggest that you read that again, only slower.

Now I need to be careful here—careful not to send the wrong message. I do not believe that people today receive audible instructions from God, receiving them directly from somewhere within their spirits. Our only reliable source of communication from God is the sixty-six books of the Bible. Some would combine the truths of Romans 8:16 and Proverbs 4:23 in dangerous ways to support their belief that God guides them with messages by "a still, small voice" from within. (We'll discover the truth about that "still, small voice" later in this chapter.)

The purpose of silence is not to receive extrabiblical instructions or secret messages from God. Yet somehow in the crucible of silence the Holy Spirit boils the truth we receive from Scripture down to its essence, reveals specific insights that are pertinent, and then applies them to our most perplexing problems and our most stubborn misconceptions. As He transforms our heart to beat more truly for Him, our decisions accomplish His will as we reflect His character.

Sustained periods of quietness are essential in order for that to happen. Our responsibility is to pursue time away from television noise, radio chatter, endless and silly commercials, and the din of mercenary traffic around us. Alone and quiet, in that place of stillness and solitude where we protect and guard our hearts with all diligence from the clamor of a world that would pollute it, God will lead us to springs of life bubbling from somewhere deep within.

I encourage you to experience this for yourself. Open the Word of God in a peaceful place and sit in quietness before Him. Let the random bits of mind-litter blow through your consciousness and wait . . . and read . . . and meditate. In time the Spirit of God will illumine a passage,

You will discover as you "cease" that your greatest problems start to shrink before Almighty God.

and it will come to life in your mind. Virtually before you know it, the knotty situation that drove you to distraction will unravel. You will discover as you "cease" that your greatest problems start to shrink before Almighty God. He will reveal Himself. He will calm your emotions and relieve your mind. You will discover new direction, freedom from worry, a sense of peace. And like the psalmist you will find Him "a very present help in trouble."

THE MINISTRY OF SILENCE

Henri Nouwen wrote these penetrating words in his book *The Way of the Heart:*

> We are now left with the question of how to practice a ministry of silence in which our word has the power to represent the fullness of God's silence. This is an important question because we have become so contaminated by our wordy world that we hold to the deceptive opinion that our words are more important than our silence. Therefore it requires a strenuous discipline to make our ministry one that leads people into the silence of God.[7]

One of our main problems is that in this chatty society, silence has become a very fearful thing. For most people, silence creates itchiness and nervousness. Many experience silence, not as full and rich, but as empty and hollow. For them silence is like a gaping abyss which can swallow them up. As soon as a minister says during a worship service, "Let us be silent for a few moments," people tend to become restless and preoccupied with only one thought: "When will this be over?"[8]

Calling people together, therefore, means calling them away from the fragmenting and distracting wordiness of the dark world to that silence in which they can discover themselves, each other, and God. After all, silence of the heart is much more important than silence of the mouth.[9]

In our chatty world, in which the word has lost its power to communicate, silence helps us to keep our mind and heart anchored in the future world and allows us to speak from there a creative and recreative word to the present world. Thus silence also can give us concrete guidance in the practice of our ministry.[10]

I do not believe anyone can ever become a deep person without stillness and silence.

I can think of few things more unappealing than a shallow ministry. Real people living in a real world with real questions as they face real trials need more than empty platitudes and a neatly trimmed theology. Anyone engaged in Christian ministry—and that should include all of us—must be a person of depth if he or she hopes to be effective. The gospel, from the lips of a shallow person, sounds hollow and insipid. But that same message uttered by a person whose waters run deep—whose intimacy with the Almighty transcends the need for an answer to every question—compels a curious world to look beyond the superficial.

I do not believe anyone can ever become a deep person without stillness and silence.

THE MINISTRY OF SOLITUDE

If silence has a mate, it must be solitude. Put them together to cultivate serenity—a peace and contentment inside that others see as confidence and security on the outside. Jesus personified serenity.

Though He was God, as a man He experienced all of humanity's limitations and temptations—including physical and mental fatigue. While on earth, He overcame the weakness of His humanity by making solitude a priority.

The gospel by Mark is an action-packed account of Jesus's life and ministry. Over and over, Mark used the words *kai euthys,* "and immediately," to string together the stories about Jesus. This happened, *and immediately* that happened, *and immediately* the other happened, all in rapid succession. Scan just the first chapter of his account to find the words repeated no fewer than ten times (1:10, 12, 18, 20, 21, 28, 29, 30, 42, and 43).

Jesus was a man on a mission, and His ministry was virtually constant. Lives were converted, the sick were healed, demons were exorcized, the blind received sight—relentless activity. The structure of the narrative suggests that all of the events described in chapter 1 occurred in a single day, and by the end the whole city was at the door (v. 33).

After such a nonstop day of ministry, notice what Jesus did: "In the early morning, while it was still dark, Jesus got up, left the house, and went away to a secluded place, and was praying there" (v. 1)

This was a perfect time for Jesus to go into Capernaum and pick up a copy of the *Jerusalem Times,* grab a cup of coffee, hobnob with His adoring public, maybe have several committee meetings with town officials to discuss the kingdom of God. But He didn't do any of that. Insecure people need to stay busy; they need the constant attention of a fawning multitude. Unless that changes, they will forever be shallow, underdeveloped people in positions of leadership. Put in charge but utterly ill-equipped to lead.

I can scarcely think of a time when I learned something significant in a crowd, surrounded by the talk and noise of even well-meaning people. I'm anything but reclusive. I love being with people . . . but not all the time. I learned that people (especially talkative people) can be draining. In solitude, though, the only person needing anything is you, and you've brought your need to God's inexhaustible supply. There He sifts the essentials of life from the chaff and trains your mind on what's important, leaving you with a healthy perspective of who you are and what He's called you to do.

"In the early morning, while it was still dark. . . ." Why so early in the morning? Was Jesus a morning person, as we would say today? Not necessarily. Early morning was probably the only time He could be alone. Even as a busy man, He found a way to balance the demands on His time with His need for solitude. Often that requires creativity and a willingness to inconvenience yourself, to the point of losing sleep, if necessary. But even making that sacrifice, there's no guarantee you'll get all of the time alone that you would prefer. Jesus sought solitude while everyone sought Him!

> Simon and his companions searched for Him; they found Him, and said to Him, "Everyone is looking for You." [Jesus] said to them, "Let us go somewhere else to the towns nearby, so that I may preach there also; for that is what I came for."
>
> —MARK 1:36–38

Expectations can be terribly frustrating. Were it anyone but Jesus, I imagine the immediate reaction would have been, "Ugh! Can't I have just a few moments alone with my Father without half the world hunting me down? Fine! What do you want from me *now?*"

But no. Look at His response. He said, in effect, "Let's go. I'm here to preach, so let's get after it." Solitude and ministry exist in tension with one another, yet they cannot be separated. Effective spiritual leaders must learn the discipline of keeping themselves in proper balance. Our purpose, like that of Christ, is to serve others, not to cloister ourselves away in order to hoard up spiritual treasures for our own enrichment.

In terms of ministry, solitude is an investment—one that will make us richer in order to share that wealth with others. On the other hand, a pauper has no riches to give. Fail to seek out solitude, and you will be too poor to give anything away. Your spiritual reservoir will stay near empty. The refreshment Jesus gleaned from solitude with the Father translated into ministry. Eventually the habits He developed became the basis for training His disciples to carry on the work after Him. What He modeled in the first chapter of Mark's gospel, He then taught in chapter 6.

Fast-forward to the scene where Jesus sent the disciples out to preach, heal, and cast out demons. Armed with the supernatural power to do what He had been doing, they witnessed great success. They got the job done. We don't know how long they were gone, but a diversion in Mark's narrative suggests that it must have been an extended period. Could have been days, perhaps a few weeks. At the end of their own busy time of ministry, look at what Jesus did:

> The apostles gathered together with Jesus; and they reported to Him all that they had done and taught. And He said to them, "Come away by yourselves to a secluded place and rest a while." (For there were many people coming and going, and they did not even have time to eat.) They went away in the boat to a secluded place by themselves.
>
> —MARK 6:30–32

Back with their Mentor, these twelve are probably elbowing each other out of the way to tell their stories and unload their questions. They're exhilarated and exhausted at the same time, flying high on the success of their ministry. Observing this, Jesus wisely said, "Whoa, wait. Stop for a minute. Get in the boat. Let's go somewhere quiet, away from everyone. You're going to get caught up in all of that if you're not careful. Let's get alone to put all of this into perspective." You can't help but wonder if He had Psalm 46 on His mind: "Cease!"

As the late Vance Havner once said, "If you don't come apart, you will come apart."

LISTEN

In truth, some of you reading this are on the ragged edge because you are continually in motion, constantly in the presence of needs and people and demands, expectations, children pulling at you, spouse needing support, friends wanting help, groups looking for a volunteer, schedules, making plans, attending events. You can't remember the last time you were absolutely alone, sitting—or better, kneeling—in silence. You've lost perspective and you're going to come apart. Believe me, I know.

When I was young and foolish, I used to say along with my equally foolish seminary friends, "I'd rather burn out than rust out!" How incredibly stupid. Either way, you're "out"!

Since then, I've read missionary biographies—glowing, sentimental tributes to an all-out, short-lived career in ministry—and wondered, *Why didn't these people take better care of themselves?* They pushed themselves beyond exhaustion and frequently died of curable or treatable diseases. Short, brilliant careers that affected a lot fewer people than if they had lived longer. Why would anybody desire either to burn out or rust out? Both options are bad. Not much ministry gets done from a pine box.

And since when is burning out so impressive? Fizzling is worse than rusting. Near the end you're tense, angry, needy, self-absorbed, demanding, resentful, and—big surprise—doing more harm than good in the cause of Christ. If Jesus Himself refused to rush on, if Jesus took time to be alone, if Jesus pulled His men away for times of solitude way back then, why do we think it's any less important for us to do the same today?

Solitude doesn't require much effort or time. And seclusion with God doesn't have to be a superspiritual setting, either. Sometime it's a motorcycle ride for me. Or a drive along the back roads in my pickup. Other times, a long and quiet walk all alone with my thoughts is best. For you, time alone with God can take any form you like, so long as you're deliberately away from other people.

Now, I can almost hear the questions.

What do I do once I'm alone?

Simple answer: listen. You'll hear things that you may have been missing.

One of my favorite questions to ask people who live up in the mountains is, "Do you hear the wind whistling through the trees?" They'll typically return a blank look, and then pause for a moment. "Oh, yeah. How about that?" Obviously, though they live in that quasi-pristine setting, they haven't listened for a long time.

Just standing on a mountain slope won't necessarily help you hear the wind in the trees, though. You have to listen for it.

What will I hear?

In a word, clarity.

Give it some time. Your mind will flood with silly cares and useless observations. Usually the longer it's been and the busier you are, the longer it will take for your mind to calm down and grow quiet. Don't fight it. Don't rush it. And don't feel guilty. It's normal. Just let your mind run. Eventually, without trying and before you know it, your mind is still. Not empty; just quiet. And the things you have studied, the lessons you have learned, the Scripture you have read or memorized, the prayers you have begun to pray will start to mingle and finally jell. The silly will be displaced by the significant. Confusion and chaos will be displaced by meaningful thoughts. Shallow will disappear as depth finds its way in.

Some like to call what they hear "a still, small voice." The phrase comes from a story about Elijah in 1 Kings 19. The tough, old prophet had just defeated the prophets of Baal on Mount Carmel and on foot had outrun the royal chariot to the palace. Enraged, the evil queen Jezebel threatened to have him killed. Elijah ran for his life, far away. Exhausted and depressed, he fell down under a tree in the wilderness and wept. "O LORD, take my life, for I am not better than my fathers" (1 Kings 19:4).

As he rested and ate, he listened for the voice of God. A whirlwind. An earthquake. A raging fire. Elijah trained his ear on each, but he heard no voice. Finally he heard what many translations call a gentle wind; the old King James Version renders it poetically "a still small voice" (v. 12).

> Wind, earthquake and fire manifested themselves in succession, but God is said not to have been in any of these. Then a different phenomenon followed. The translations *a gentle whisper* and "a still small voice" (RSV) do not do full justice to the enigmatic Hebrew expression, which may be better rendered "a brief sound of silence."[11]

The Hebrew word is usually found in poetic writing. "Several times in the Psalms this verb is used of being still before the Lord in quiet meditation."[12] In other words God spoke audibly to Elijah out of silence as the prophet waited all alone. It was in that place of solitude that God connected with His servant. Elijah heard with his ears, not his spirit. He literally heard God's message.

We will hear from God, though not in the same way. We are not prophets relaying new information from God to His people. We have available to us all the information we need. As I mentioned earlier, it's all there between the covers of our Bible. And we have the indwelling Holy Spirit to teach us using our experiences, the advice of godly counselors, and the information handed down via the prophets and apostles. Nevertheless, we must listen . . . in quietness. As we find solitude, the still, small voice we hope to hear will be a sense of clarity as we allow the Holy Spirit to transform our thinking.

PRESERVE WHAT YOU DISCOVER

I have found that one of the best uses of my time in solitude is to keep a journal. Merriam-Webster defines *journal* as "a record of experiences, ideas, or reflections kept regularly for private use."[13] A journal is not merely a record of how you're spending your time; it's actually a record of your spiritual journey. A journal isn't to be confused with your calendar, your organizer, or even a diary. To keep it from becoming shallow, I recommend that you avoid writing in it every day.

If you've never used a journal, you may wonder how to start. Easy, really. Open it to the first page, put your pen to the paper, and write the very first thing that comes to mind. This isn't an essay contest. No one will grade you. In fact, no one will see it but you. (More on that later.) You aren't required to write anything profound. Just write. In that place of solitude, let the words begin to flow. Perhaps you can start by writing a brief prayer to your heavenly Father.

I gave a student who was graduating from Dallas Theological Seminary a journal and encouraged him to record some of the valuable things the Lord would reveal to him during his first year out of seminary. He later told me what he wrote as his first line: "I have never journaled before, so this is a new experience for me." He went on to fill two pages in that first sitting, including a few brief, very personal prayers.

A journal is an exercise in which the process, not the product, is the most important result. That's why I do not recommend using a computer. Word processing programs make editing very easy, and if you want to craft literature, that's the tool to use. Editing is precisely what you want to avoid with a journal. Pour your thoughts onto paper, by hand, without concern for grammar or spelling or punctuation, without worry or apology, without thinking about how it will read later. The journal is a tool to help you and the Holy Spirit make the best use of your solitude.

Keep in mind that it is *your* journal, not something you write for someone else. I do not record my journey with God with the hope that someone will publish it someday. I hope that my journals will never be made public. Yet they are part of the legacy I leave for my family after I die. These words represent my deepest thoughts. They are my best and most intimate expressions, all handwritten.

One journal ends on June 30, 1994. I wrote, *"These have been some of the toughest days of my entire life."* The next journal continues where that one leaves off—the day I began as president of Dallas Seminary. The opening words:

I'm beginning this journal July 1, 1994, the day I officially became president of Dallas Seminary. Only by Your grace, O God, have I been chosen and called to fill this position. Whatever is accomplished

will be by Your power and therefore only for Your glory. Guide me,
O Thou great Jehovah.

For a number of reasons, those were some of the loneliest days of my life. The journals I kept during that time cultivated a deep serenity in my aloneness with Him. I was often reminded of what my mother used to say: "Roots grow deep when the winds are strong."

I want that for you. Deep roots.

PURSUE THE TREASURE THAT PAUL TAUGHT

Let's conclude by returning to Paul's great goal in life:

> [For my determined purpose is] that I may know Him—that I may progressively become more deeply and intimately acquainted with Him, perceiving and recognizing and understanding [the wonders of His Person] more strongly and more clearly, and that I may in that same way come to know the power outflowing from His resurrection [which it exerts over believers]; and that I may so share His sufferings as to be continually transformed [in spirit into His likeness even] to His death.
>
> —PHILIPPIANS 3:10 AMP

Paul's "determined purpose" was to become like Christ. If we want to be like Christ, we would be wise to do the things He did. He made silence and solitude a priority, not because He disliked the people around Him or the work He was doing. While He didn't hide from people and flee responsibility, He pursued His Father.

I urge you to become more like Christ. That will happen as you pursue what He pursued. Make silence and solitude a priority. In that quiet aloneness, let the Holy Spirit cultivate serenity in you. You owe it not only to yourself but to those you love most. If you don't, you will never really know the God you worship, and your loved ones will never really know who you are.

Please . . . start today.

four

Surrender:

Releasing Our Grip

When grace changes the heart, submission out of fear changes to submission out of love, and true humility is born.[1]

—WILLIAM HENDRIKSEN

Surrender:

Releasing Our Grip

Ron Ritchie is one of a kind, a real character. I met him while I was at Dallas Seminary, and we became good friends. In fact, I often think of Ron and his ministry, for many years at Peninsula Bible Church in Palo Alto, California, then later in Colorado Springs. Shortly after I finished my four years at Dallas Seminary, I served as assistant pastor at Grace Bible Church in North Dallas while Ron had another year to complete. I was glad to have him as a friend for my first year in ministry. He had a great way of putting life into its most basic terms, which was, no doubt, one result of having to work his way through school as a custodian. (Many seminarians have had their theology seasoned by hard labor. It's all part of God's design for training His servants, preparing them to be good ministers.)

Ron gave me a perspective on ministry that I have returned to repeatedly over the years, especially when it seemed overly difficult or complicated. He often said, "Three-fourths of ministry is just showing up." That's one of the best statements I've ever heard, even after more than forty years in public ministry.

THE FAITHFUL SHOW UP

First Corinthians 4:2 says, "It is required of stewards that one be found trustworthy." Being trustworthy often means little more than showing up, simply being ready and available, in season and out of season. Paul tells us it is required of a steward that he be found *faithful*—not necessarily fruitful or full of charisma or excited or brimming with optimism, but faithful. When Satan, the world, and your own hurt feelings say, "Stay home; it ain't worth it!" God has a better plan: just show up. That's what the faithful do. They keep showing up.

In the summer of 1995, Baltimore shortstop Cal Ripkin Jr. brought the sports world to its feet by breaking a record that many people thought would stand forever—a record set by the legendary Lou Gehrig back in 1939. It was no great display of strength, speed, or accuracy. Just plain, old-fashioned faithfulness. On September 6, 1995, Ripkin showed up, again, just as he had 2,130 consecutive times before.

When Ripkin walked on the field to begin game 2,131, the ballpark thundered for twenty-two uninterrupted minutes as the crowd stood and applauded. Cal stood, too, in classic, Ripkin style, turning slowly in a circle as he looked around the stadium. Then he did something wonderful. He walked over to his family and embraced each one of them. The victory was theirs too.

What a great moment in sports history. No championship trophy, no dramatic, final-seconds triumph. This was simply a gracious, public declaration to honor a man who faithfully did his job year after year. Cal Ripkin Jr. showed up.

Showing up is one part of faithfulness—a crucial part, sometimes the hardest part. But Hebrews 12:1 reveals another side of faithfulness you may not have considered before. Let me show you something subtle yet profound in this exhortation to early Christians.

BEFORE THE FAITHFUL SHOW UP, THEY LET GO

> Therefore, since we have so great a cloud of witnesses surrounding us,
> let us also lay aside every encumbrance and the sin which so easily
> entangles us, and let us run with endurance the race that is set before us.
>
> —HEBREWS 12:1

According to the author of Hebrews, we, just like Cal Ripkin Jr.,
are surrounded by an eternal, invisible stadium full of witnesses—
spectators to witness either our victory or defeat. The "therefore"
points to chapter 11, which tells us that the stands aren't filled with
sports fans applauding us for being faithful, but with unseen people
who have gone on ahead—saints of old throughout the Old and New
Testaments, early church history, and all the way up to our own
century. Since we are surrounded by witnesses in this great arena
called Christianity, since we have surrounding us such a great cloud of
souls who have gone on before, "let us lay aside every encumbrance
and the sin which so easily entangles us, and let us run with endurance
the race that is set before us."

Take note that the race is "set before us." As is true of anyone who
runs a race, the track is not set by the runner. The path for the race is
prearranged. Competitors are disqualified if they leave their assigned
lane or wander from the prescribed course.

Next, it's worth noting that before we run the race, we are told to
get rid of every encumbrance. The Greek word *onkos* means, literally,
"weight" or "mass." Ancient authors frequently used this word picture
to represent anything that might be a burden. It could be anything,
such as excess fat or bulky clothes. Competitors in the original
Olympics sacrificed their pride to gain the slightest edge by running
completely nude!

I think the author of Hebrews deliberately left its meaning vague here. In the word picture he paints of a runner, the encumbrance is anything that slows him down and keeps him from running his fastest.

Pause for a moment. Don't leave the scene without asking yourself, "What is *my* encumbrance?"

We are also instructed to set aside "*the* sin." The Greek carefully and conspicuously includes the definite article, pointing to a particular sin, not a group of sins or all sin in general.

The King James calls it the sin that so easily "besets" us. Some take that to mean a "besetting sin" is unique to each person. One individual's besetting sin may be greed, while the besetting sin for another may be sloth. I may be frequently overcome by gluttony while jealousy may dominate you. It could be envy or lust, pride or gossip.

I don't think that's the best explanation for the author's use of the definite article. It's best to interpret the use of "the" within the context of chapters 11 and 12. Like a pin in the hinge that holds a door to its jamb, "the" links chapter 12 to chapter 11, which is full of people who truly believed God—men and women of great faith. "The sin" in Hebrews 12:1 is, most likely, *unbelief.*

Hebrews 11 has been called the Westminster Abbey of the people of God, a memorial to believers in this great hall of faith. With them in his mind the author writes, "Now, you are surrounded by a cloud of witnesses like those people I just told you about, and I challenge you to run the race God has prescribed for you. But first—before doing anything—lay aside *the* sin. Lay aside unbelief."

After careful observation of this verse, I am convinced of this: the author of Hebrews cannot conceive our successfully running life's race without first deciding to trust God—*really* relying on Him. And that kind of trust begins by surrendering to Him.

OUR GOAL REVISITED

Before moving on, let's recall the finish line. It's marked out by Philippians 3:10:

> [For my determined purpose is] that I may know Him—hat I may progressively become more deeply and intimately acquainted with Him, perceiving and recognizing and understanding [the wonders of His Person] more strongly and more clearly, and that I may in that same way come to know the power outflowing from His resurrection [which it exerts over believers]; and that I may so share His sufferings as to be continually transformed [in spirit into His likeness even] to His death.
>
> —PHILIPPIANS 3:10 AMP

We've discussed disciplines that help us reach that goal.

- Intimacy—returning to our first love by developing a close, personal walk with God.

- Simplicity—shuffling our priorities to help us reorder our lives, free our minds, and clear our lives from the clutter that spoils intimacy with the Almighty.

- Silence and solitude—slowing down, shutting out the clamor and frenzy of a frivolous world in order to allow the Spirit of God to teach our spirit.

Now we come to the toughest discipline so far: surrender. How difficult it is to release our grip! You may notice that these first disciplines involve getting rid of things: complications, clutter, noise, distractions. But all of those are unpleasant things. Who doesn't want to fling them far away? Oh, but surrender. Laying down our will. Releasing our grip on our rights, our plans, our dreams. Now we're dealing with a completely different matter. Now we're getting rid of something we love!

At the core of such thinking is a four-letter word that resists all thought of surrender: SELF.

Let's face it: most of us can talk a good fight when it comes to surrender. But I will freely confess, it is a battle royal to this day in my own life. Letting go, laying aside *the* sin: unbelief. Not so much a lack of trust in God as having such a love for my way as to miss His. We often fail to go God's way because we're so captivated by our own. I mean, we've been at this a long time. We've got this thing called life down pat, right? That's part of becoming an adult, isn't it? In truth, at the core of such thinking is a four-letter word that resists all thought of surrender: *self.*

No one understood that better than the Puritans. The following comes from a Puritan prayer titled "Man a Nothing." It's written anonymously because the words belong to anyone honest enough to claim them:

> When thou wouldst guide me I control myself,
> When thou wouldst be sovereign I rule myself.
> When thou wouldst take care of me I suffice myself.
> When I should depend on thy providings I supply myself,
> When I should submit to thy providence I follow my will,
> When I should study, love, honour, trust thee, I serve myself;
>> I fault and correct thy laws to suit myself,
>> Instead of thee I look to man's approbation,

and am by nature an idolater.

Lord, it is my chief design to bring my heart back to thee.

Convince me that I cannot be my own god, or make myself happy,

    nor my own Christ to restore my joy,

    nor my own Spirit to teach, guide, rule me.

Help me to see that grace does this by providential affliction,

    for when my credit is god thou dost cast me lower,

    when riches are my idol thou dost wing them away,

    when pleasure is my all thou dost turn it into bitterness.

Take away my roving eye, curious ear, greedy appetite, lustful heart;

Show me that none of these things

    can heal a wounded conscience,

    or support a tottering frame,

    or uphold a departing spirit.

Then take me to the cross and leave me there.[2]

SELF-INTEREST IS THE MORTAL ENEMY OF SURRENDER

So how do we surrender? How do we begin to release our grip and truly rely on God? The author of Hebrews, writing God-breathed words, gives us practical answers in the next two verses. They call for two actions. Both are antidotes to the poison that kills belief—self-interest:

Study Christ.

and

Compare yourself to Christ.

STUDY CHRIST

Hebrews 12:2 states, "fixing our eyes on Jesus, the author and perfecter of faith, who for the joy set before Him endured the cross, despising the shame, and has sat down at the right hand of the throne of God."

Read those words again, only slower this time. Picture the words in

As the author and finisher of our faith, He not only designed the course of the race; He ran it.

your mind. We start to practice the discipline of surrender when we focus our eyes on the person of Christ. The word picture of a race is retained in this verse. Did you notice? We might be tempted to think that Jesus is just the finish line and that we should only keep our eyes on Him as a runner would focus on the tape. But I think the author is urging us to also think of Jesus as the *example.* As the author and finisher of our faith, He not only designed the course of the race; He ran it. In fact He ran it perfectly. As the first verse says of us, He too had a course set before Him. Furthermore running it necessarily involved surrender. As our example Jesus modeled trust in the Father. He came to the planet that He had made and lived His entire life misunderstood, misrepresented, misquoted, mistreated, and finally crucified. Yet He committed no sin. From Bethlehem's manger to Golgotha's cross, Jesus exemplified a life of surrender.

The Greek term *aphoraō* at the beginning of verse 2 means to look exclusively at something and study it intently while consciously looking away from distractions. And the implication is imitation. Great athletes study the films of former greats to discover their techniques, to uncover any secrets to success that might offer even the slightest competitive edge. We are encouraged to go to the film vault and peer intently at one scene after another as we study Christ. "Look exclusively and thoughtfully at the One who not only designed the course but ran it flawlessly. Then run exactly as He ran." As He lived, we are to live. As He decided, we are to decide. As He obeyed, we are to obey. As He pleased the Father, we are to please the Father. As He surrendered, we are to surrender.

Here's the good news: when we live surrendered lives before Him, becoming like Him leads to the ever-increasing reality. We don't have to pray for it. We don't have to strive to accomplish it. Focusing intently on Christ naturally results in a lifestyle of greater and greater selflessness. As you read earlier, practicing the discipline of surrender begins with selflessness.

Paul wrote to his Christian friends in Philippi while he was under house arrest in Rome, hoping to convince them to imitate Christ's selflessness. In Philippians 2:3–5, he gave them four commands: the first and the third are negative; the second and the fourth are positive. He then held up Christ as the ultimate example. He modeled the discipline of surrender to such a degree that sacrifice was inevitable. Here are the commands:

1. Do nothing from selfishness or empty conceit (v. 3).

2. With humility of mind regard one another as more important than yourselves (v. 3).

3. Do not merely look out for your own personal interests (v. 4).

4. [Look out] also for the interests of others (v. 4).

Did you notice? The second command leads off with four significant words: "with humility of mind." In Matthew 11:29 Jesus called

Himself "gentle and humble in heart," using the same root word, *tapeinos,* meaning lowly or of low social standing. Someone who accepts his place at the bottom of the social order has no self-serving expectations. He leaves no room for selfishness.

You want to be like Christ? Begin by thinking of yourself as lowly. Deliberately work toward becoming unselfish. For one full day, let go of anything that serves your own interest to the exclusion of others. On that same day, fix your attention on Jesus by surrendering in complete selflessness. By doing this you will follow a divinely ordained plan that is not your preference.

Don't miss the precise wording of the third command. I'm glad the editors of the New American Standard Bible included "merely" in their translation. You can't live so entirely selflessly that you never look out for your own interests. No one—not even God—expects you to become the local doormat. Obviously, failing to seek adequate food, shelter, clothing, and other necessities would be foolish. Keep all of this in balance. It's a question of priorities and emphasis. "Not *merely* your own personal interests, but *also* for the interests of others."

Eugene Peterson's *The Message* paraphrases this nicely in modern terms: "Don't push your way to the front; don't sweet-talk your way to the top. Put yourself aside, and help others get ahead. Don't be obsessed with getting your own advantage. Forget yourselves long enough to lend a helping hand" (Philippians 2:3–4 MSG)

Following the four commands, Paul points to Jesus as the perfect illustration of selflessness. Read the following very carefully, preferably aloud:

Have this attitude in yourselves which was also in Christ Jesus, who, although He existed in the form of God, did not regard equality with God a thing to be grasped, but emptied Himself, taking the form of a bond-servant, and being made in the likeness of men. Being found in appearance as a man, He humbled Himself by becoming obedient to the point of death, even death on a cross. For this reason also, God highly exalted Him, and bestowed on Him the name which is above every name, so that at the name of Jesus every knee will bow, of those who are in heaven and on earth and under the earth, and that every tongue will confess that Jesus Christ is Lord, to the glory of God the Father.

—PHILIPPIANS 2:5–11

Jesus "did not regard equality with God a thing to be grasped." Though Jesus deserved all the respect, all the worship, all the adoration, all the fear due Him as God, He let it all go. He released His grip on all of it.

Further, "He emptied Himself." While retaining every aspect of His deity, Jesus relinquished the independent use of His divine attributes during His earthly sojourn. Before the Son became a flesh-and-blood man, He had absolute autonomy as God, being coequal, coeternal, and coexistent with the Father. When He became a man, He voluntarily gave up the independent use of His divine attributes; and while on this earth, He submitted to the Father. He waited on the Father for His will, for His timing. He followed the Father's guidance as to where He would go and what He would do and what He would say and when He would do those things. He relinquished the voluntary use of His divine prerogatives. He gave up what was rightfully His for the sake of others—including you and me.

Moreover, He took "the form of a bond-servant" and was made "in the likeness of men." He did this so that He could suffer "a cross-kind of death" (the Greek sentence suggests such a rendering.) The excruciating, humiliating anguish of a common criminal became His kind of death.

Imagine! Thirty-three years after leaving the absolute, indescribable beauty and freedom and perfection of heaven, He hung between thieves on rugged timbers with spikes through His hands and feet, with human saliva dripping from His face and blood flowing from lacerations that covered His body from head to foot. In death He personified surrender.

The Son of Man gave up His will for the Father's. As a result, the Father glorified Him.

Is it any wonder, then, that the author of Hebrews encourages us to fix our eyes on Jesus, to focus our gaze on Him, to study Christ? Focusing intently on Christ naturally results in a lifestyle of increasingly greater selflessness. And it has another benefit. Gazing on Christ gives us greater ability to look past life's trials and remain calm in the midst of what others would call chaos. Remember the old chorus?

> Turn your eyes upon Jesus,
> Look full in His wonderful face;
> And the things of earth will grow strangely dim
> In the light of His glory and grace.[3]

It's true. Somehow fixing your eyes on Jesus causes other things to dim in significance. Possessions, people, reputation, opinions, political rhetoric, world wars, death, disease, heartache—all of these and so much more grow strangely dim when we gaze on Him.

COMPARE YOURSELF TO CHRIST

Hebrews 12:3 prescribes a second action that will help us overcome the self-interest that undermines the discipline of surrender: "For consider Him who has endured such hostility by sinners against Himself, so that you will not grow weary and lose heart."

"Consider Him" in verse 3 and "study Him" in verse 2 sound the same, but they are not. The English terms used by most translations fail to emphasize the distinction that appears so clearly in the Greek. The term used in verse 3 in the original language is *analogizomai*, an accounting term. You do this every time you balance your checkbook. You compare your figures against those of the bank, and because banks rarely make an error, you usually adjust your totals to match the statement. It's a careful, logical analysis involving comparison.

"Study" carries the idea of fixing your attention exclusively on Christ for the sake of understanding; "compare" calls for you to measure yourself against His experience and His example.

The next time you're feeling sorry for yourself, pause long enough to compare your situation to His. The next time you're unfairly criticized, again, compare; weigh your trouble against what He endured. The next time you have to surrender something comfortable or something familiar for a greater good, compare what you are surrendering to what He surrendered. The next time you're asked to adjust to a plan, compare your adjustment to His adjustment.

Keep Jesus as your standard. All other human examples are driven by a survival instinct, an internal compulsion to preserve and nurture self. Only Christ modeled godly selflessness throughout His entire life. While others seek to preserve their own lives, He came to lay His down.

What's the benefit? Look again at the verse. "[Compare, then imitate] Him who has endured such hostility by sinners against Himself." Why? "So that you will not grow weary and lose heart."

Ever notice how much energy it takes to keep a tight grip on something? Let go. You won't grow weary; you won't get worn out if you release your grip. Some of you reading this today already know what you're holding on to. Your emotions are in turmoil because you cannot avoid the inevitable. You've been clutching it far too long and, sooner or later, your grip will fail and it will be lost anyway. It's a problem too great for you to solve, a responsibility too heavy for you to shoulder, or perhaps even a blessing that has come to dominate your every waking thought. Rather than have it ripped from your weary, cramped fingers, choose to release it into God's care. You're not simply letting it drop; that's giving in to defeat. You're releasing it to One greater than yourself and trusting—believing—that He is both able and willing to care for it better than you.

Release your grip. Stop resisting and simply surrender. You'll be amazed by how much more energy you will have, how much more positive your attitude will become, how much easier life will be to live.

Release your grip. Stop resisting and simply surrender. You'll be amazed by how much more energy you will have, how much more positive your attitude will become, how much easier life will become. The decision to surrender may feel a little like suicide. Satan would have you think that releasing your desires to the Father will end your life—or at least your happiness. That fear can be debilitating. Perhaps that's why some picture the decision to trust God as a leap.

Once you make the choice, the hardest days are the earliest. You have become so accustomed to carrying a great weight that releasing it will naturally upset your balance. Learning to walk without it will feel awkward at first. Keep your eyes fixed on Christ and walk slowly. As you regain your balance over time, you'll be amazed by the growing intimacy you share with Him, your example. You're living as He did, you're sharing His experience, and you know Him better than ever . . . He's right there by your side. In fact He is within you, urging you to take your next step.

Let me warn you again. Surrender is tough at the start, especially if you are a selfish kind of person, a little spoiled, a little pampered, a little overly indulged. Your old self will whine and fight for survival! Surrendering is not for the pampered. God honors those who pay the price to be like Him: selfless. That's why surrendering plays such a dominant role in putting self in its place.

THINGS TO SURRENDER

Before turning to some areas of life for specific application, pause for a moment to ponder Proverbs 3:5–8. We too easily take the wisdom of Solomon for granted. Sometimes his familiar advice can appear trite if we're not careful. Given all that we have discussed, his words of wisdom fit well here. Read these lines slowly several times:

> Trust in the LORD with all your heart,
> And do not lean on your own understanding.
> In all your ways acknowledge Him,
> And He will make your paths straight.
> Do not be wise in your own eyes;
> Fear the LORD and turn away from evil.
> It will be healing to your body,
> And refreshment to your bones.

SURRENDER YOUR POSSESSIONS

Now is a perfect time for you to put your possessions into proper perspective. If you're married, do this with your partner. Make a list of any material possessions that you know are near and dear to your heart. Then go before the Lord with your list. Release them one by one—by name—to

Him. Declare Him the owner of each item. As you surrender your possessions to Him, you will find a sense of freedom and relief from materialism and greed like you've never known before. You may be surprised by how much you idolized those possessions without realizing it. If you find your heart especially close to a particular item, you might consider making it a literal gift to God. Give it to someone who needs it more than you and therefore could put it to better use. The sacrifice will sting initially—sacrifices always do!—but in time you might be surprised to discover the Lord trusting you with more than you originally had.

I don't mean to suggest that poverty is somehow more spiritual than wealth. It is not. In fact, God's purpose in giving Israel the Promised Land was to bless them with such material abundance that the nations would take notice and inquire about Him. However, it is also true that if you don't hold the possessions you own loosely, they will own you. And so, enjoy them . . . but refuse to idolize them! That's not an easy balance, even for those who don't wrestle with greed.

In his wonderful book *The Pursuit of God* A. W. Tozer concludes the second chapter, "The Blessedness of Possessing Nothing," with this powerful prayer:

> Father, I want to know Thee, but my cowardly heart fears to give up its toys. I cannot part with them without inward bleeding, and I do not try to hide from Thee the terror of the parting. I come trembling, but I do come. Please root from my heart all those things which I have cherished so long and which have become a very part of my living self, so that Thou mayest enter and dwell there without a rival. Then shalt Thou make the place of Thy feet glorious. Then shall my heart have no need of the sun to shine in it, for Thyself wilt be the light of it, and there shall be no night there.[4]

We'll never become like Christ as long as possessions mean more to us than they should.

SURRENDER YOUR POSITION

Release your grip on the top rungs of your career and/or social ladder. Stop wrapping your ego around your role. This is especially difficult for pastors. Too many identify themselves so closely with their ministry that it bears their name. Should the Lord move them to something else, a large part of them dies. The same is often true of executives and successful business owners. I have seen this happen to mothers as well. Deliberately refuse to allow any position or title to determine who you are. *Let it go!*

*F*ind your security, your identity, and your contentment in God.

Release the title, release the position, release the benefits, the perks, your own importance or power, whatever goes with it. Place it all before your God. Find your security, your identity, and your contentment in Him.

SURRENDER YOUR PLANS

Come now, you who say, "Today or tomorrow we will go to such and such a city, and spend a year there and engage in business and make a profit." Yet you do not know what your life will be like tomorrow. You are just a vapor that appears for a little while and then vanishes away. Instead, you ought to say, "If the Lord wills, we will live and also do this or that." But as it is, you boast in your arrogance; all such boasting is evil.

—JAMES 4:13–16

I am convinced that wise planning is good. But plans, like material possessions, must always be held loosely. Yes—always! Plan wisely, but be ready for God to rearrange things and take you along paths that may feel dangerous to you. Don't sweat it; He knows what He's doing. And He isn't obligated to inform you . . . or request permission to upset your neat little agenda!

SURRENDER YOUR PEOPLE

Hold the people you love loosely. I'm thinking especially of your children, your parents, your friends who mean so much to you. Accept the fact that nothing this side of heaven is permanent, including relationships. If they don't end, they will certainly change. Enjoy the time you have with your loved ones but avoid the temptation to cling.

This is especially difficult with your children. Believe me, after releasing four of my own, I know. If you haven't already, go before the Lord and commit each one by name to Him. Thank Him for allowing you to nourish those precious lives, ask His guidance to do the job well, and give each one to Him for whatever He wills. Then prepare yourself for the day when you must release them into the world and His care. I should warn you, He may very well choose to take one of them before you're ready. So releasing each one now will make the premature parting more bearable.

Wyatt Prunty's poem "Learning the Bicycle" paints a familiar picture for most parents and has a great deal to teach us:

LEARNING THE BICYCLE
(for Heather)

> The older children pedal past
> Stable as little gyros, spinning hard

To supper, bath, and bed, until at last
We also quit, silent and tired
Beside the darkening yard where trees
Now shadow up instead of down.
Their predictable lengths can only tease
Her as, head lowered, she walks her bike alone
Somewhere between her wanting to ride
And her certainty she will always fall.
Tomorrow, though I will run behind,
Arms out to catch her, she'll tilt then balance wide
Of my reach, till distance makes her small,
Smaller, beyond the place I stop and know
That to teach her I had to follow
And when she learned I had to let her go.[5]

Older parents understand that all too well. Part of the thrill of guiding children into adulthood is the release. But it's also a parent's greatest act of surrender. Still, you have to let them go. Start now.

SURPRISES AWAIT YOU

Finally I want to share two observations from my personal experience and my experience as a pastor. I am so confident in the truth of these that I dare call them principles. If I may go one step further, I suggest you memorize both of these statements:

Surrender results in surprises we would never otherwise experience.

and

The greater the struggle to surrender, the greater the surprise.

I urge you. Release your grip. Surrender it all to God, including your anxiety. If you still have your emotions wrapped around some issue involving a possession, a job or role, a particular expectation for the future, or a relationship, you aren't fully relying on God. As long as you fail to surrender to Him, you're holding on to anxiety. Stop. Let go. You're delaying the surprise God has waiting for you.

Peter Marshall, the late chaplain of the United States Senate, concluded a message on anxiety titled, "Sin in the Present Tense," with this prayer. I leave it with you to make it your prayer today.

Forgive us, O God, for the doubting suspicion with which we regard the heart of God.

We have faith in checks and banks, in trains and airplanes, in cooks, and in strangers who drive us in cabs. Forgive us for our stupidity, that we have faith in people whom we do not know and are so reluctant to have faith in Thee who knowest us altogether.

We are always striving to find a complicated way through life when Thou hast a plan, and we refuse to walk in it. So many of our troubles we bring on ourselves. How silly we are.

Wilt Thou give to us that faith that we can deposit in the bank of Thy love, so that we may receive the dividends and interest that Thou art so willing to give us. We ask it all in the lovely name of Jesus Christ, our Savior.[6]

five

Prayer:

Calling Out

Prayer is listening as well as speaking, receiving as well as asking; and its deepest mood is friendship held in reverence. So the daily prayer should end as it begins—in adoration.[1]

—GEORGE A. BUTTRICK

Prayer:

Calling Out

UNDERSTANDING PRAYER

Understanding any spiritual discipline begins with a good defini-
tion. Put succinctly, prayer is communicating with God. A conversation that can be spoken or silent, and even expressed in song. Many of
the psalms are prayers set to music. A primary purpose of prayer is
connecting with God in order to transfer His will into your life. It's
colaboring with God to accomplish His goals.

Prayer is a vital expression of trust in the Lord that emerges from
our devotion and commitment. E. M. Bounds put it this way: "When
the angel of devotion has gone, the angel of prayer has lost its wings,
and it becomes a deformed and loveless thing."[2]

Prayer often involves other disciplines such as meditation, worship,
silence, solitude, and surrender—always surrender.

Effective prayer will have a believer deliberately seeking the mind
of God on a particular matter that's on his or her heart. Whether it's
confessing a sin or praising His name or pursuing His will or inter-
ceding for a friend or petitioning for our own needs, prayer must be

God-centered, never self-centered. Sincere prayer comes from a heart that longs for God to reveal what He desires. So prayer must also allow adequate time for listening, waiting intently before the Father.

God never hides His will. If we seek direction, He delights in providing it.

WHAT PRAYER IS NOT

Since prayer is one of the most powerful of all spiritual disciplines, we shouldn't be surprised that it is among the most misunderstood as well. Christian prayer has some important distinctions from the discipline in other religions, yet it's a temptation for Christians—even those who have known the Lord for years—to make prayer complicated. It is easy to have a distorted perspective.

While He was on earth, Jesus clearly addressed what should be avoided when His followers pray:

> When you pray, you are not to be like the hypocrites; for they love to stand and pray in the synagogues and on the street corners so that they may be seen by men. Truly I say to you, they have their reward in full. But you, when you pray, go into your inner room, close your door and pray to your Father who is in secret, and your Father who sees what is done in secret will reward you. And when you are praying, do not use meaningless repetition as the Gentiles do, for they suppose that they will be heard for their many words. So do not be like them; for your Father knows what you need before you ask Him.
>
> —MATTHEW 6:5–8

Prayer is not bargaining or pleading. As Douglas V. Steere, a Quaker scholar, wrote, "It's not a question of changing God's mind or of exercising some magical influence or spell."[3] Pagan religions worshiped gods that could be charmed with incantations and influenced by offerings. But attempts to coerce God didn't stop with ancient rituals; they are ever-present among us! "Name it and claim it" until your face turns blue, sow all the "seeds of faith" until your checkbook gasps, but God will not be manipulated. Jesus opened the way for us to have direct access to the throne of heaven—an awesome privilege that would have boggled the minds of the Old Testament saints. To reduce prayer to a cheap marketing scheme insults God's character. He is holy and righteous, and He will always act in your best interests whether you behave correctly or not.

To reduce prayer to a cheap marketing scheme insults God's character. He is holy and righteous, and He will always act in your best interests whether you behave correctly or not.

Prayer is not a get-rich-quick scheme. Despite what many of the media hucksters may tell you, prayer does not release the powers of good fortune from heaven, filling your pocketbook with an abundance of cash. Difficult as it is to understand, His will may be for His people to live as poor as dirt, just as His own Son and the apostles who followed Him did.

Prayer is not presenting God with a wish list as though He were a genie. Neither is prayer a laborious, painful marathon of monotonous misery entered into for hours each day to prove one's piety to God. It is not the repetition of the same religious words. Remember? Jesus condemned "meaningless repetition." On the contrary, rather than trying to motivate or impress God to gain what we want, prayer is an authentic seeking of His plan as we willingly adjust *our* will to match His.

WHAT PRAYER IS

Prayer is one's personal conversation with the Almighty that includes both expressing our concerns and listening to His response. Our hope in doing so is to glean His perspective, or as Paul called it, "the mind of Christ" (1 Corinthians 2:16). Thankfully we can have this conversation anywhere and at any time.

Prayer is one's personal conversation with the Almighty that includes both expressing our concerns and listening to His response.

It takes me about twenty-five minutes early on Sunday mornings to drive from our home in Dallas to Stonebriar Community Church in Frisco. It takes much longer during the week. Usually I leave the radio off in order to use that time for prayer. I'll walk through the morning message in my mind and ponder snags that emerge in the sermon. I'll ask for guidance on how to transition between complex points or how to illustrate a difficult truth. I'll also talk with Him about special needs, like how to blend the worship service that morning into a meaningful service of praise or ask His guidance regarding some matter of church business, easily switching back and forth between large and small issues.

I pray for my wife. I pray for all four of our children. I pray for our ten grandchildren, mentioning each one before the Lord. I pray for Dallas Theological Seminary, our government leaders, and sometimes for world affairs—tragedies, conflicts, or efforts for peace. I am often amazed by how many concerns I'm able to cover during a short twenty-five-minute drive in silence.

Often I speak to God out loud. Sometimes I sing to Him. Occasionally the entire prayer will be in my mind. Each time I commit myself to using that time for prayer, I notice that God becomes my focus rather than some personal struggle. I am relieved of worry. I am able to release anything concerning me so that I could become altogether lost in the majesty of His presence and the joy of ministry. When I arrive, I'm excited to do as God pleases. I find myself refreshed, relieved, and ready. My mind is focused. My heart is prepared. My emotions are clear, and whatever was troubling me when I began that drive no longer concerns me. Prayer has made that possible.

Now, I wish that I could say that I use *every* commute every day for time in prayer. But, like many people, I often forget. My mind will be spinning from one problem to the next and rather than pray, I churn. At times I'll be so anxious that it doesn't occur to me that I should quit worrying and commence praying. (More about worry in a moment.)

THE PRIORITY OF PRAYER

Prayer is not a natural response; it's a Spirit response. If we fail to cultivate this discipline, prayer winds up being our last resort rather than our first response. Sometime after Timothy became the pastor in Ephesus, Paul wrote him a letter of instruction. In the second chapter of 1 Timothy, Paul communicated to his son in the faith many of the fundamentals of ministry. Not surprisingly he started with the discipline of prayer, beginning with the words, "First of all . . ."

> First of all, then, I urge that entreaties and prayers, petitions and thanksgivings, be made on behalf of all men, for kings and all who are in authority, so that we may lead a tranquil and quiet life in all godliness and dignity.
>
> —I TIMOTHY 2:1–2

Note the priority Timothy was admonished to give to prayer. In effect, Paul wrote, "First of all, I urge you. I plead with you, Timothy, *first* pray. *First,* before you slide out of bed. *First,* before you take a shower to start your day. *First,* before you make your way to work. *First,* before any appointment. *First of all,* pray, pray, pray."

Long before Paul wrote Timothy, we are able to see how important prayer is to building a ministry by returning to the amazing growth of the first church in Jerusalem. In the very beginning, according to Acts 2:42, the first Christians devoted themselves to four essentials: "They were continually devoting themselves to the apostles' *teaching* and to *fellowship,* to the *breaking of bread* and to *prayer*" (emphasis added).

We could call these the four corners of a church foundation. No church is complete without all four. Leave out any one of them and you may have a school, a prayer group, a Bible study, or a social gathering—and each of those is a good thing—but you won't have a church. The church in Jerusalem was established and sustained on prayer.

Shortly after the new church in Jerusalem began, Peter and John were busy in their day, yet the text tells us that they were "going up to the temple at the ninth hour" (Acts 3:1). Three o'clock in the afternoon was the hour of prayer for Jews. The apostles took time in the middle of their afternoon to attend a gathering for the purpose of prayer.

But this didn't stop the pressure that was mounting against those early Christians. Matter of fact, those early believers began to experience such intense persecution, some were thrown into jail. Prayer went up for them. When they were released, their companions again "lifted their voices to God with one accord" (Acts 4:24) as they prayed for the success of the gospel and the faithfulness of the church. Their first response to persecution was not panic; it was prayer. They interrupted the course of events to seek God's mind, to plead for His protection, to ask for His strength and sustaining grace.

Ben Patterson, chaplain at Westmont College, wrote, "That's what prayer does, says the Lord. It's radical, it goes down deep beneath the surface to uproot evil and upset the status quo."[4] When your day is rolling along at its own pace and in its own direction, interrupt it with prayer. As your day builds toward a crisis, deliberately stop to pray. When your morning begins to go south, pull away for a few moments of solitude to seek God's mind and ask for His instruction. When your attitude starts to sour, pause for an attitude adjustment, prompted by prayer. Don't wait—pray immediately.

The church that started (Acts 2) and grew through persecution (Acts 4–5) kept multiplying. Acts 6 describes a church that had grown so large in size and in responsibility—the members numbered in the multiple thousands—that the apostles could not meet all the needs. For example, some widows weren't getting the food they needed in order to survive, so the twelve recognized the need for a radical change. They urged the congregation to select qualified people to handle this and other practical matters. Once done, they delegated several duties to those men in order to keep their priorities straight as the spiritual leaders of the congregation. "But we will devote ourselves to prayer and to the ministry of the word" (6:4). Wise decision. The needs were addressed and dealt with, allowing the apostles to stay with their priorities.

I am especially fortunate to serve in a church whose elders are mature spiritual leaders. Their dedication to prayer reveals their maturity. Our meetings are punctuated by times of prayer. We begin by praying and then dive into general matters of the church only to realize it's time once again . . . time for more prayer. We may see matters on the agenda that are beyond our ability to handle, so we lay them before the Lord in prayer. We stop everything to spend at least fifteen to twenty minutes each meeting in prayer as each one of us comes before the Lord with specific concerns.

This would probably seem like a huge waste of valuable time to a corporation. Some might say, "You can't keep doing that; you've got a church to run." No. Actually, we don't. It's not *our* church; it's God's—and it's not our responsibility to run it! Fortunately He is responsible for the church's success, however that should be defined. Our priority is to devote ourselves to prayer and to the ministry of the Word. In the end, we find that our time praying is an investment that pays for itself many times over. When each elder or pastor has his will aligned with the Lord's, we waste no time arguing for our own. It's amazing what effect prayer has on our relationship with one another. Barriers are broken down. Hearts are softened. Wills become submissive. And fresh ideas flow freely.

Stonebriar Community Church is sustained by prayer. Behind the scenes are prayer groups meeting to intercede on behalf of the church, sometimes scheduled in advance and other times completely spontaneous. During a typical day, an e-mail or a phone call will come in representing a need, and almost without exception, the one who presents the need to me will say, "We have to stop right now and pray over this." And we'll pray right then. Some needs are so grave or so urgent that several of us will gather during the day for prayer. And I wouldn't have it any other way. Our commitment as spiritual leaders in the church is, first of all, to be people dedicated to prayer and to the ministry of the Word.

Acts 7 recounts a tragic day in the life of the first church. Enemies of the gospel dragged Stephen, a deacon, before a mock court and condemned him to die by stoning. As the stones crushed him, he prayed, "Lord, do not hold this sin against them!" (v. 60). Standing nearby, a man held the robes of Stephen's brutal executioners. His name was Saul, later called Paul.

Saul had seen firsthand the results of prayer in building a movement he couldn't destroy. Stephen's prayer quite probably haunted him. Enraged, perhaps by conviction, Saul multiplied his efforts to destroy every Christian he could find. But the Lord disabled him on the road to Damascus and made him a champion of the very movement he tried to wipe out—the movement built and sustained by prayer.

No wonder he told Timothy, "First of all, pray!"

THE CURE FOR WORRY

May I get very personal here? The pressures of our times have many of us caught in the web of the most acceptable, yet energy-draining sin in the Christian family: worry. Chances are good you awoke this morning, stepped out of bed, and, before doing anything, strapped on your well-worn backpack of anxiety. You started the day, not with a prayer on your mind but loaded down by worry. What a dreadful habit!

Jesus challenged His followers with the question, "And who of you by being worried can add a single hour to his life?" (Matthew 6:27). Worry solves nothing. It creates unrest, uneasiness, and, left unchecked, it can churn our waves of anxiety into a perfect storm of emotions. Add a little imagination and creativity, and our worst fears come to life in Technicolor brilliance.

The stress from worry drains our energy and preoccupies our minds, stripping us of our peace.

The stress from worry drains our energy and preoccupies our minds, stripping us of our peace. Few in God's family are exempt. We fret over big things and little things. Some of us have a laundry list of concerns that feed our addiction to worry. It's a very unattractive addiction, yet we somehow manage to make a joke out of it. I've heard people say with a smile, "If I don't have something to worry about, I get worried about not having something to worry about." Anxiety has become a favorite pastime that we love to hate. And worse, we're passing it on to our children. As they see the worry on our faces and they hear it from our lips, we're mentoring them in the art of anxiety.

PRAY WITHOUT CEASING

As always, Scripture has the answer. Paul, again, is the writer. Hoping to relieve the anxiety of his friends in Philippi, he wrote from his imprisonment:

> Rejoice in the Lord always; again I will say, rejoice! Let your gentle spirit be known to all men. The Lord is near. Be anxious for nothing, but in everything by prayer and supplication with thanksgiving let your requests be made known to God. And the peace of God, which surpasses all comprehension, will guard your hearts and your minds in Christ Jesus.
>
> —PHILIPPIANS 4:4–7

His prescription for anxiety can be boiled down to this:

Worry about nothing. Pray about everything.

Wait.

Before moving on, read those six words again slowly, several times. Notice that the remedy to worry involves a choice. He's not asking you to exist in a state of denial. "Don't worry; be happy" fails to appreciate the seriousness of the concerns you have. You worry because the problems you face are difficult to solve. Furthermore they have grave consequences if you don't find a resolution. God doesn't expect you to suddenly stop caring. Instead He offers an alternative to the pointless and exhausting habit of worry: "Be anxious for nothing, but in everything by prayer and supplication with thanksgiving let your requests be made known to God" (Philippians 4:6).

Before this day is done, you will have another occasion to choose between worry and prayer. Determine now what you will do. Decide now that when the crisis arises you will transform the worry into prayer. If at the end of praying, your emotions are still in turmoil, pray more. By cultivating the discipline of prayer, you will discover the ability to remain calm and quiet. As you wait before the Lord, you'll find relief from fear's grip on your spirit.

Worry is wrestling with anxiety on your own rather than releasing it to the Father.

You might be tempted to think that your prayer was ineffective or that you somehow failed because your anxiety returned—perhaps as soon as you said, "Amen." Happens all the time to me. I take my persistent anxiety as a signal that I need more time before the Father, reviewing all the details of my problem, telling Him how much it plagues me, and sometimes even admitting that I'm afraid He won't handle it soon enough. Having a deep, persistent concern for a problem is not the same as worry. Worry is choosing to fret and churn instead of turning it completely over to God. Worry is wrestling with anxiety on your own rather than releasing it to the Father.

Most people whom I consider to be men and women of prayer go before God because their hearts are heavy. They tell me that nothing but continual conversation with Him brings them relief. So if you tend to worry a lot, here's a better plan: pray a lot. For such relief to become a reality, you will have to exercise the discipline of surrender as you rely on Him to solve the problem . . . in His way and in His time. Effective, results-getting prayer includes the thought, *Lord, this is Your problem to fix. You take control. Let me know what You want me to do if I'm to be involved in the solution. By leaving it with You, I will consider it solved.* It's at that point you discipline your mind not to worry, not to continue seeking answers or trying to find resolution. You solved the problem by giving it to God. Your major responsibility now is to wait for His leading. When He wants you to act, He will make it clear. He has dozens of ways to do that, so there's no need for me to open that door. As you wait before Him, He will direct your thoughts to the next step you should take. If there is nothing He leads you to do, do nothing more. He will take it from there.

Because we are weak creatures of habit, our anxiety will quite likely return and we will have to return to prayer and release it all again. That's normal. In fact, if we could rid ourselves of all anxiety with a thirty-second prayer, 1 Thessalonians 5:17 wouldn't make much sense: "pray without ceasing."

Start your day with prayer and continue praying off and on through the day. Pray as you drive. Pray at work. Pray before your lunch break. Pray when you get that difficult phone call. Pray when you are disappointed by something. Pray when surprises come. Pray when you triumph. Pray in the midst of painful news. Pray without ceasing . . . *literally*. Your heavenly Father, being touched deeply over your struggles, loves it when you come to Him, asking for help. He is right there, ready to step in. Invite Him to do just that!

LET HIS PEACE FILL YOU

Prayer is classic proof that we don't master spiritual disciplines easily. Developing the discipline of prayer while breaking the habit of worry will call for great mental effort. It will take time for you to master this new way of thinking. Stay with it. After persistent, continual conversation with the Father, mixed well with waiting for Him to work, you will receive what has been promised you. After doing your part, God will do His. Count on it!

"And the peace of God, which surpasses all comprehension, will guard your hearts and your minds in Christ Jesus" (Philippians 4:7). Inexplicable peace will replace inner churning. Tranquility that seems to come from nowhere will envelop your mind. It will begin to take over other parts of your life.

In his fine book, *The Spirit of the Disciplines,* Dallas Willard describes how this happens:

> Praying with frequency gives us the readiness to pray again as needed from moment to moment. The more we pray, the more we think to pray, and as we see the results of prayer—the responses of our Father to our requests—our confidence in God's power spills over into other areas of our life. Out of her vast experiences with prayer in the harrowing life of a missionary wife and mother, Rosalind Goforth explains: "Perhaps the most blessed element in this asking and getting from God lies in the strengthening of faith which comes when a definite request has been granted. What is more helpful and inspiring than a ringing testimony of what God has done?"[5]

COMMON PERILS AND UNCOMMON PROMISES

We began this chapter by addressing what prayer is and isn't. A good way to end it is with a few thoughts on what we can and cannot expect from a life of continual conversation with God. First some common misconceptions and mistakes that I have seen among well-meaning Christians; then a few promises from God to encourage you.

THE PERIL OF IRRESPONSIBILITY:
SUBSTITUTING PRAYER FOR RESPONSIBLE ACTION

Prayer is never a substitute for human responsibility.

Make no mistake here. Prayer is never a substitute for human responsibility. Imagine a seminary student, preparing for a lifetime of teaching and preaching the Word of God, getting ready for an exam. As the date approaches, he begins to pray, *Lord, help me score well on the exam.* Every day he gets on his face before God and pleads for the ability to do well, but he never once cracks a book. He is faithful to pray, but he fails to prepare. In situations like that the Lord will do at least this during the test: He will help the student bring to mind all that he studied!

Very often God has granted us the privilege of contributing to the answer to our own prayers. So don't merely pray about losing weight, exercise! Don't merely hope that someone helps meet the needs of the impoverished, give! By all means, pray for your friends who do not know Christ, but tell them about the free gift of salvation! Take your concerns about your children before the Lord, but don't forget to listen to them! Divine intervention and human involvement often work hand in hand.

THE PERIL OF MISPERCEPTION: PICTURING GOD AS MERELY SUPERHUMAN

I remember thinking as a little boy that God is eight hundred years old, looks like a great-great-granddad, has a long, white beard, and is very powerful but essentially is like a kind, old man. Ridiculous! What's worse, do you know what that does to prayer? It shackles God with all the limits of humanity.

Your view of God will shape every aspect of your spiritual life, especially how you pray. It will determine what you pray for, the peace (or lack of such) you will glean from the discipline, and greatly impact what you expect God to accomplish. The truth is, He is limitless in power and His capabilities are far beyond our imagination. Do your prayers reflect an awesome, sovereign God or merely a kind, old man?

THE PERIL OF OVERCOMMITMENT: POSTPONING PRAYER DUE TO A BUSY SCHEDULE

When you're too busy, prayer gets squeezed out of the schedule.

J. Sidlow Baxter once shared a page from his own pastoral diary with a group of pastors who had inquired about the discipline of prayer. He began telling how in 1928 he entered the ministry determined he would be the "most Methodist-Baptist" of pastors, a real man of prayer. However, it was not long before his increasing pastoral responsibilities and administrative duties and the subtle subterfuges of pastoral life began to crowd prayer out. Moreover, he began to get used to it, making excuses for himself.

Then one morning it all came to a head as he stood over his work-strewn desk and looked at his watch. The voice of the Spirit was calling him to pray. At the same time another velvety voice was telling him to be practical and get his letters answered, and that he ought to face up to the fact that he was not one of the "spiritual sort"—only a few people could be like that. "That last remark," says Baxter, "hurt like a dagger blade. I could not bear to think it was true." He was horrified by his ability to rationalize away the very ground of his ministerial vitality and power.[6]

Prayer is an investment. The time you dedicate to prayer isn't lost; it will return dividends far greater than what a few moments spent on a task ever could.

THE PERIL OF OVERSIMPLIFICATION:
REDUCING PRAYER TO SHALLOW FORMULAS

God isn't a vending machine. Yet, too often we come to Him hungry and ready to trade our sacrifices for whatever will fill our need. Popular televangelist figures would have us believe that we're still hungry because we didn't pray correctly. We weren't specific in our asking. We didn't demonstrate faith with a sacrifice. We didn't pray with enough belief. We didn't claim promises, or use the right words, or have the right attitude, or . . . or . . . or. . . . They would have us think that without the right formula, God will not act on our behalf—that He withholds His goodness until we approach Him using the right ritual.

God is a true and very real being, not an impersonal force. Prayer is a vital part of our relationship with Him. The faith we exercise in prayer is not in seeing specific results for specific requests, but an expression of trust in our almighty, loving Father who cares for us and knows, better than we, what we need.

Martin Luther used to have "table talk" lectures with his students. During one of those sessions, this is what he told them about prayer:

To be sure, all of the churches across the land are filled with people praying and singing, but why is it that there is so little improvement, so few results from so many prayers? The reason is none other than the one which James speaks of when he says, "You ask and do not receive because you ask amiss" (James 4:3). For where this faith and confidence is not in prayer, the prayer is dead.

From this it follows that the one who prays correctly never doubts that the prayer will be answered, even if the very thing for which one prays is not given. For we are to lay our need before God in prayer but not prescribe to God a measure, manner, time or place. We must leave that to God, for he may wish to give it to us in another, perhaps better, way than we think is best. Frequently we do not know what to pray as St. Paul says in Romans 8, and we know that God's ways are above all that we can ever understand as he says in Ephesians 3. Therefore, we should have no doubt that our prayer is acceptable and heard, and we must leave to God the measure, manner, time and place, for God will surely do what is right.[7]

So much for the bad news. Enough of perils! Here's the good news; three promises to help you pray.

GOD PROMISES THAT HE WILL HEAR AND ANSWER REGARDLESS OF THE TIME

And how bold and free we then become in his presence, freely asking according to his will, sure that he's listening. And if we're confident that he's listening, we know that what we've asked for is as good as ours.

—I JOHN 5:14–15 MSG

God is never too busy, never sleeps, never has His mind so occupied with running the universe that He will not hear you. And yet, never forget that an answer to prayer doesn't mean that He will solve our problems the way *we* want them solved. But He will hear our requests and respond with solutions—sometimes surprising ones—that not only address our concerns but deepen our faith in His wisdom and strengthen our confidence in His sovereignty.

GOD PROMISES HIS PRESENCE
REGARDLESS OF THE OUTCOME

God wants good things for every son and daughter, and He wants to bless us, but never at the expense of our holiness. He may choose to deny our request for one blessing if the refusal paves the way for a greater one. Paul, no doubt, was terribly disappointed and frustrated when God refused a reasonable request:

Because of the extravagance of those revelations, and so I wouldn't get a big head, I was given the gift of a handicap to keep me in constant touch with my limitations. Satan's angel did his best to get me down; what he in fact did was push me to my knees. No danger then of walking around high and mighty! At first I didn't think of it as a gift, and begged God to remove it. Three times I did that, and then he told me,

"My grace is enough; it's all you need.

My strength comes into its own in your weakness."

Once I heard that, I was glad to let it happen. I quit focusing on the handicap and began appreciating the gift. It was a case of Christ's strength moving in on my weakness. Now I take limitations in stride, and with good cheer, these limitations that cut me down to size— abuse, accidents, opposition, bad breaks. I just let Christ take over! And so the weaker I get, the stronger I become.

—2 CORINTHIANS 12:7–10 MSG

In time he discovered that God had given him something greater than relief from pain. He denied what Paul wanted in favor of what Paul needed—a greater sense of God's presence. Paul shared this painful story with his Christian disciples in Corinth to assure them that God will do the same for all believers.

GOD PROMISES INNER PEACE AND RELIEF
REGARDLESS OF THE CHAOS AND COMPLICATION

Remember the outcome God promised as a result of continual prayer?

Before you know it, a sense of God's wholeness, everything coming together for good, will come and settle you down. It's wonderful what happens when Christ displaces worry at the center of your life.

—PHILIPPIANS 4:7 MSG

What does the Lord provide in place of worry? A transcendent peace. A tranquility that others can't understand. They'll look at you, calm in the middle of a raging storm that life has rained down on you, and say, "How can you possibly smile at a time like this?" And your answer will be, "I have no idea—except to say that my hope is in the Lord. God is good, He is in control, and I will be fine in the end." Few thoughts bring greater comfort.

God's goal for us is intimacy with Him. I have discovered, however, that the cultivation of intimacy can get complicated. That happens when our will gets in the way of seeking His. Richard J. Foster put it well:

> Nothing is more central to the spiritual life than prayer, for prayer ushers us into perpetual communion with the heart of God. And there are many things to learn about this life of constant conversation with the Holy One.
>
> But we must beware of making things too complicated. Like children coming to their parents, so we come to God. There is awe to be sure, but there is also intimacy. We bring our heart cries to a loving Father. Like the mother hen who gathers her chicks under her wings, so our God cares for us, protects us, comforts us (Matt. 23:37).
>
> So no matter how much we study the labyrinthine realities of prayer, let us forever come as children to a loving Abba who delights to give and to forgive.[8]

Our primary goal in calling out to God throughout a life of prayer is not to make our daily existence easier or more enjoyable for ourselves—although, from a certain point of view, it will. The goal can be summed up in four words: intimacy with the Almighty. Seek that first, and you will have everything you've longed for in life, including all the things you never knew you needed.

six

Humility:

Bowing Low

Humility must always be the portion of any man who receives acclaim earned in the blood of his followers and the sacrifices of his friends.
—DWIGHT D. EISENHOWER

Humility:

Bowing Low

Discipline is something no one likes but everyone admires. Discipline is something that great women and men exhibit behind closed doors, away from admiring fans and cheering crowds. Discipline is hard work done in obscurity for the sake of excellence. And I have noticed that disciplined people are almost always humble. They don't need cheering crowds to feed their hunger for excellence.

Discipline gives birth to great musicians. Jascha Heifetz, perhaps the greatest violinist of the twentieth century, first picked up his instrument when he was three years of age. He practiced four hours every day of his life, right up to his death at eighty-seven. Do the math. That's more than one hundred thousand hours of practice in private, punctuated by occasional one-hour performances in public.

The great Italian painter and Renaissance man Leonardo da Vinci desired nothing less than anatomical perfection for his paintings, and he spent countless hours studying the human body. For one commission, he became so frustrated by his inability to paint the body as he wished that he drew a thousand hands until he felt it was just right.

Centuries later we gaze in awe at his paintings and forget the hours of preparation. We're barely aware of the diligent training of da Vinci's hand, mind, and heart for the sake of those magnificent canvas images.

At barely six feet tall and just a little over two hundred pounds soaking wet, Mike Singletary didn't look much like a linebacker. But after ten appearances in the NFL Pro Bowl and landing a spot in the Pro Football Hall of Fame, few would deny that the former Chicago Bears linebacker was among the very best to play the game. He broke tackling records almost as often as he broke helmets—equipment managers routinely brought no fewer than three for each game. He was also very precise; he always knew where the ball would be so he could be there to meet whoever carried it. All of that came from intense preparation—physical and mental. Hours, after others had gone home, Singletary studied the films of opposing teams and trained tirelessly in the weight room. All for only sixty minutes on the playing field, fewer than twenty times a year.

We love great music. We admire magnificent art. And we envy the coordination and the skill of superb athletes. But how easy it is to forget that it's the discipline we didn't see that made the gifted musicians, the creative artists, and the superb athletes the best at what they did and made them worthy of admiration and respect.

I like the word picture Dallas Willard paints of a teenager wanting to mimic his hero on the ball field:

Think of certain young people who idolize an outstanding baseball player. They want nothing so much as to pitch or run or hit as well as their idol. So what do they do? *When they are playing in a baseball game,* they all try to behave exactly as their favorite baseball star does. The star is well known for sliding head first into bases, so the teenagers do too. The star holds his bat high above his head, so the teenagers do too. These young people try anything and everything their idol does, hoping to be like him—they buy the type shoes the star wears, the same glove he uses, the same bat.

Will they succeed in performing like the star, though? We all know the answer quite well. We know that they won't succeed if all they do is try to be like him in the game—no matter how gifted they may be in their own way. And we all understand why. The star performer himself didn't achieve his excellence by trying to behave in a certain way *only during the game.* Instead, he chose an overall life of preparation of mind and body, pouring all his energies into that total preparation, to provide a foundation in the body's automatic responses and strength for his conscious efforts during the game.[1]

What's true of musicians, artists, and athletes is all the more true among the godly. If you have known an individual whom you respect because of his or her spirituality, you can be certain that person has cultivated the disciplines of godliness. He or she wasn't born that way. The life you respect and hope to emulate didn't automatically come with age or a promotion to some position. You can be sure that the person you admire paid dearly for his or her spiritual depth—hours of trying, failing, and trying again; suffering through hardship; learning to rely on God; yielding to the spiritual disciplines because he or she finds that life works better that way. Paul encouraged Timothy, his protégé, "Discipline yourself for the purpose of godliness" (1 Timothy 4:7).

*G*odliness has one very important difference when compared to music, art, and athletics. Unlike those pursuits, godliness has no public performance in mind.

Godliness has one very important difference when compared to music, art, and athletics. Unlike those pursuits, godliness has no public performance in mind. That's especially true for the discipline of humility, for humility forbids grandstanding. If anyone else notices, it is incidental. We pursue the spiritual disciplines for an audience of One. Remember our goal?

> [For my determined purpose is] that I may know Him—that I may progressively become more deeply and intimately acquainted with Him, perceiving and recognizing and understanding [the wonders of His Person] more strongly and more clearly, and that I may in that same way come to know the power outflowing from His resurrection [which it exerts over believers]; and that I may so share His sufferings as to be continually transformed [in spirit into His likeness even] to His death.
>
> —PHILIPPIANS 3:10 AMP

HUMILITY IS NOT MERELY A VIRTUE; IT'S A DISCIPLINE

As we focus our thoughts on the discipline of humility, let's begin by clarifying four important issues, just to get on the same page. I feel the need to do this because many people consider humility a virtue, not a discipline. Indeed, humility *is* a quality of one's character, but it's more. Much more.

First, *although humility is a Christlike virtue, it is neither understood nor admired by most Western cultures.* Most models of strong leadership consider it rather strange for a prominent leader to show humility. Bending the knee to help others or to admit weakness is to make oneself vulnerable to those who would displace him. Leaders usually view themselves as being there to be served, except for short periods of time when it's noble to condescend and serve others—but not for too long. He must be careful not to associate too closely with those lower on the ladder or he will compromise his own position. She might lose the respect of her subordinates *and* her superiors if she accepts too much responsibility for a poor decision.

Not so in the culture of Christ! Humility is not something a person merely has; it's what we are called to *do*.

Second, *we appreciate humility in others but rarely want it for ourselves.* The price is too high. Humility is not what gets us ahead, and—let's be completely honest—we like humble people around us because they don't threaten our position. They're safe people with that quaint little virtue that keeps them on the sidelines during the scramble to the top of the hill. We can afford to be humble *after* we're king. Even Christ's disciples weren't immune, as seen in the following scripture. Note the Lord's response:

> [The disciples and Jesus] came to Capernaum; and when He was in the house, He began to question them, "What were you discussing on the way?" But they kept silent, for on the way they had discussed with one another which of them was the greatest. Sitting down, He called the twelve and said to them, "If anyone wants to be first, he shall be last of all and servant of all."
>
> —MARK 9:33–35

If we see humility as a discipline, not merely a virtue, we better understand the task before us. It has more to do with what we seek than what we become. If we take responsibility for what we seek, God will determine what we will be.

Third, *humility is not the result of having low self-esteem.* There are some who would have us focus our full attention on our own unworthiness, our pitiable estate and wormlike qualities, justifying such a mind-set by adding that we amount to nothing apart from Christ. I don't argue with the truth of any of those perspectives, but they don't nurture humility. That's not how Jesus came by His. When He was on earth, He had no sense of inferiority. He never struggled with insecurity. How could He? He was God!

Phillip Yancey coauthored with Dr. Paul Brand some of the most compelling books I have ever read, among them *Fearfully and Wonderfully Made* and *The Gift of Pain*. The late Dr. Brand was one of the twentieth century's greatest, most respected physicians because of his selfless care for those who suffer from leprosy. His love for India's least of the least led him to make discoveries that centuries had overlooked and to pioneer surgical techniques that surgeons use today in orthopedic reconstruction. He was a brilliant physician, medical teacher, writer, speaker, and champion for discarded people. Here's what Yancey had to say about him:

> Meeting Dr. Brand, I realized that I had misconstrued humility as a negative self-image. Paul Brand obviously knew his gifts: he had finished first throughout his academic career and had attended many awards banquets honoring his accomplishments. Yet he recognized his gifts as just that, *gifts* from a loving Creator, and used them in a Christlike way of service.
>
> When I first met him, Brand was still adjusting to life in the United States. Everyday luxuries made him nervous, and he longed for a simple life close to the soil. He knew presidents, kings, and celebrities, yet he rarely mentioned them. He talked openly about his failures and always tried to deflect credit for his successes to his associates. Most impressive to me, the wisest and most brilliant man I

have ever met devoted much of his life to some of the lowest people on the planet: members of the Untouchable caste in India afflicted with leprosy.[2]

No, humility isn't a result of having a poor self-image. True humility comes from a place of strength and inner security. Genuinely humble people who have a desire to seek the well-being of others are generally very secure people. They are fully aware of their gifts, their training, their experience, and all the attributes that make them successful at whatever they do. That security—that honest, healthy self-assessment—results in more than a humble constitution; it translates into actions that can be observed, actions that we will want to emulate.

Genuinely humble people who have a desire to seek the well-being of others are generally very secure people.

The elder President Bush praised Ronald Reagan's humility in his eulogy. In 1981, Reagan was recovering from the gunshot wound he received during the assassination attempt. Just days after the surgery that repaired his life-threatening injuries, his aides discovered him on his hands and knees in his hospital room, wiping water from the floor. Bush said of Reagan, "He worried that his nurse would get in trouble."

I call that gracious act of humility strength of character. How rarely would we imagine our president on his hands and knees cleaning up his own mess. But that's true humility. Not merely a quality of a great woman or man, but an action for which the most natural posture is on all fours.

Fourth, *as a discipline we can measure our success in humility. As a virtue we cannot.* As soon as we think we're humble, we're not! Samuel

Taylor Coleridge and Robert Southey wrote in 1799, "And the devil did grin, for his darling sin is pride that apes humility." I have found that genuinely humble people have a natural inattention concerning their humility. They don't even think of themselves as humble. As a matter of fact, they rarely think of *themselves* at all. Humble people are too occupied with the well-being of others to guard their own interests or notice their own self-importance. J. Steven Wilkins wrote in his fine work, *Call of Duty: The Sterling Nobility of Robert E. Lee:*

> The degree to which [Lee] was indifferent to his own honor is astonishing. After the war, Lee often received distinguished visitors from the North into his home in Lexington. Assuming that the Lees, like many prominent families in the North, had household servants, the guests, after retiring to bed would often leave their boots and shoes outside their bedroom doors to be cleaned and "blacked." Many a night it was the general who stayed up after all others had retired and—in order not to embarrass his guests—collected the boots and cleaned and polished them himself.[3]

THREE LESSONS IN HUMILITY

Have I convinced you? We can only pursue humility as an action, a behavior, not as a quality of character. And yet, if we exercise the discipline long enough, it will inevitably dominate our nature without our knowing what happened. We will become oblivious to it. Unfortunately the transformation in our character won't happen automatically or easily or quickly. So what does the exercise of this discipline look like? Scripture provides at least three good examples to study. Each one illustrates a key principle.

HUMILITY STARTS AT THE BOTTOM

I wish being around humble people would automatically make us humble. The disciples provide adequate proof that it doesn't. Mark 10:35–45 describes an incident involving James and John, two brothers. The situation will make most parents nod and smile. By the way, this is the same John who wrote the book of Revelation, the Gospel of John, and the three letters that bear his name. This episode, of course, took place before he grew into maturity—still a disciple, still young, and still looking out for John:

> James and John, the two sons of Zebedee, came up to Jesus, saying, "Teacher, we want You to do for us whatever we ask of You." And He said to them, "What do you want Me to do for you?" They said to Him, "Grant that we may sit, one on Your right and one on Your left, in Your glory." But Jesus said to them, "You do not know what you are asking. Are you able to drink the cup that I drink, or to be baptized with the baptism with which I am baptized?" They said to Him, "We are able." And Jesus said to them, "The cup that I drink you shall drink; and you shall be baptized with the baptism with which I am baptized. But to sit on My right or on My left, this is not Mine to give; but it is for those for whom it has been prepared." Hearing this, the ten began to feel indignant with James and John. Calling them to Himself, Jesus said to them, "You know that those who are recognized as rulers of the Gentiles lord it over them; and their great men exercise authority over them. But it is not this way among you, but whoever wishes to become great among you shall be your servant; and whoever wishes to be first among you shall be slave of all. For even the Son of Man did not come to be served, but to serve, and to give His life a ransom for many."

—MARK 10:35–45

So, You Want to Be Like Christ?

These two sound like a couple of kids with their daddy, don't they? "Dad, we want to ask you a favor and we want you to say yes. We want you to do whatever we ask, okay? Promise?" And don't miss what they wanted. They hoped that when Jesus eventually defeated the Romans and was crowned king of Israel, He would put His loyal followers in key positions of power. In a royal court the chair to the right of the king was reserved as the highest place of honor and authority. The next in line sat to his left. James and John didn't want to remove Jesus from His rightful place on the throne, but they had no desire to serve anyone else!

Most Christians can identify with that kind of raw ambition. We're happy to follow and obey Jesus, but we loathe to submit to a fellow human being who might abuse his or her authority. It's hard enough to submit to Jesus, who's perfect. Giving up our comfort or position for the sake of another sinner is far more difficult.

I find it interesting that Jesus didn't rebuke James and John's lust for power. I love His response to their request, His classic way of cutting to the chase. Abruptly He responded, "You don't know what you're asking." The seats next to Jesus in the kingdom of God aren't filled on a first-come, first-served basis. Certainly the most ambitious don't get the nod. In the kingdom, suffering brings reward, and positions of authority come at the expense of selfless sacrifice. "The cup" was a familiar Jewish metaphor that could refer either to joy or judgment for sin. In this case it was both. "Baptism" was a common word picture in Old Testament literature for someone who was overwhelmed by tragedy and sorrow. Jesus was thinking of His own suffering and humiliating death, and He invited the two disciples to join Him in His destiny.

Does that invitation sound familiar? Let me remind you: "[My determined purpose is] that I may know Him and the power of His resurrection and the fellowship of His sufferings, being conformed to His death" (Philippians 3:10).

But they still didn't connect the dots. When He asked them, "Are you able to do this?" their naive reply betrayed their ignorance. "We're able," they answered, probably thinking that He was asking them to fight at His side in the battle to claim the throne of Israel. Jesus granted at least part of their request. He promised that they would share in His unjust punishment and agonizing death for the sake of others.

The response of the other ten disciples is predictable. The Greek term Mark used to describe their emotion tells us they were all incensed, outraged; we would say, "ticked off." The other disciples had every reason to be angry, but I wonder at what specifically. Angry at the audacity of James and John for being so brazen about their ambition? Or angry because the two had taken a more direct route to what each of them secretly wanted for himself? Perhaps both. I think especially the latter.

Jesus took the opportunity to do a little mentoring. He used the occasion to contrast the kingdoms the disciples had seen on earth and the kingdom He would bring. In the world's culture, leadership is defined by high-ranking positions and the exercise of authority, power, and dominion over other people. The words "exercise authority" that Mark used refers to a forced subduing of one person by someone more powerful. This is not someone merely taking charge; this is aggressive domination. That's the picture of authority in the first-century Roman world—and ours to a great extent.

Our modern world is run by chain of command. In the corporate world there are executive vice presidents, vice presidents, managers, and superintendents. In the military, generals command colonels, who command majors, who command captains, and so on all the way down to the lowly private at the end of a mop handle. The first lesson you learn in boot camp is that your sergeant outranks you, and from 3:00 a.m. to well after sundown for twelve weeks, he'll never let you forget it. The protocol is simple. Do whatever he says to do . . . or else. That's "overlording." That's the way the system works—and don't you forget it!

Jesus barely took a breath after contrasting the two kingdoms and added, "not so among you." The "not so" part of the Greek sentence appears first to make it emphatic. Not so in kingdom life! There's no status. There's no privileged rank. The lowly don't pamper the privileged. Quite the opposite in Jesus's kingdom. Once He got their attention, He spelled out the details:

> Whoever wishes to become great among you shall be your servant; and whoever wishes to be first among you shall be slave of all. For even the Son of Man did not come to be served, but to serve, and to give His life a ransom for many.
>
> —MARK 10:43-45

Notice the verbs "to serve" and "to give." In effect the Lord said to His disciples, "In my kingdom, godliness starts at the bottom." What was true then is true now. You want to be like Christ? Find the least desired position, the task no one else wants, the worst seat in the house, and claim it. Make it yours.

William Barclay writes, "The basic trouble in the human situation is that men wish to do as little as possible and to get as much as possible. It is only when they are filled with the desire to put into life more than they take out, that life for themselves and for others will be happy and prosperous."[4] The kingdom is built on the foundation of selflessness with Jesus as the cornerstone. The world doesn't need more prima donnas. The world longs to find servants—authentic, humble-hearted servants. Let's not litter the landscape with more pride.

Rudyard Kipling was a favorite of mine in high school. His poem "Mary's Son" is appropriate here:

MARY'S SON

> If you stop to find out what your wages will be
> And how they will clothe and feed you,
> Willie, my son, don't you go on the Sea,
> For the Sea will never need you.
>
> If you ask for the reason of every command,
> And argue with people about you,
> Willie, my son, don't you go on the Land,
> For the Land will do better without you.
>
> If you stop to consider the work you have done
> And to boast what your labour is worth, dear,
> Angels may come for you, Willie, my son,
> But you'll never be wanted on Earth, dear![5]

The sobering conclusion to this vignette in Mark 10 is that not one of the twelve disciples had a clue. All twelve failed to understand, after everything they had recently seen and heard. They went on with their day without so much as a glimpse of the entirely new way of thinking that Jesus had just presented and had been modeling ever since they met Him. Obviously humility is not something that comes merely by associating with humble people.

At the risk of being overbearing, let me urge you not to be so callous as to miss the point: "If anyone wishes to come after Me, he must deny himself, and take up his cross and follow Me" (Mark 8:34). Talk about saying it straight!

So, You Want to Be Like Christ?

Mark wrote of an event that occurred in the lives of the disciples where their lack of humility prompted a selfish lust for power. Paul encouraged the Philippian Christians to answer Jesus's call to selflessness so they would enjoy unity—a quality no congregation can enjoy without members who consistently pursue the discipline of humility. The disciples in the church at first-century Philippi lacked humility of mind—that habitual selflessness that comes by consistently putting others ahead of self.

Philippians 2:3–11 forms two segments of Paul's exhortation on humility: a command and a perspective to help his readers obey it. In verses 3–4, Paul commands humility while describing what the discipline would look like among the believers:

> Do nothing from selfishness or empty conceit, but with humility of mind regard one another as more important than yourselves; do not merely look out for your own personal interests, but also for the interests of others.
>
> —PHILIPPIANS 2:3–4

What difference does the discipline of humility make in a community? I can think of at least four important results. First, Christians remove selfishness as a motivation. Second, they become less conceited. Third, believers think of others as more important than themselves. Fourth, they deliberately and consistently attend to the needs of others.

In verses 5–11 the apostle provides a perspective that should spark feelings of gratitude. In the chapter on surrender, I suggested Paul used these words to highlight Jesus as a model worth emulating. I also think he used this example of Jesus's selfless sacrifice to drive us to our knees:

Have this attitude in yourselves which was also in Christ Jesus, who, although He existed in the form of God, did not regard equality with God a thing to be grasped, but emptied Himself, taking the form of a bond-servant, and being made in the likeness of men. Being found in appearance as a man, He humbled Himself by becoming obedient to the point of death, even death on a cross. For this reason also, God highly exalted Him, and bestowed on Him the name which is above every name, so that at the name of Jesus every knee will bow, of those who are in heaven and on earth and under the earth, and that every tongue will confess that Jesus Christ is Lord, to the glory of God the Father.

—PHILIPPIANS 2:5–11

As you read that passage, did you notice the downward trend?

Christ Jesus existed in the form of God,
  did not clutch His equality with God,
    emptied Himself,
      took the form of a slave,
        became a man,
          humbled Himself,
            and became obedient to death,
              even a cross kind of death.

What begins in the glories of heaven ends with the worst kind of death—the cruelest, most shameful mode of execution ever devised by mankind: crucifixion. Paul reminds us that Jesus chose this voluntary downgrading so that He might one day lift us up.

What is it that prompts humility within me? What do I need to think or to do that will allow me to think less of myself and more of others? A full appreciation for the sacrifice that Christ made for me will do that. Everything I have, everything I am, every good thing I enjoy would not be possible were it not for Him. The more I understand the price He paid, the less room I have for pride. The more I comprehend how Christ humbled Himself and served me, the more I'm able to put my needs below those of others. I exist because of the price another has paid.

On May 29, 2004, veterans of World War II gathered in Washington, D.C., for the dedication of the memorial to the men and women who served in that great conflict. When so many of the veterans were interviewed, several Medal of Honor winners were among them. I heard a consistent theme emerge from those who had earned our nation's highest military honor. It wasn't pride. I detected no spirit of entitlement or expectation of special treatment. There was no bitterness or cynicism over how long it took our country to build that monument. Neither did I see lingering anguish, although many cried over the names of the dead heroes. Throughout the four-day dedication and celebration, I witnessed enormous gratitude . . . and especially humility. Why? Because they naturally go together.

Dwight Eisenhower said it best shortly after Germany's surrender in 1945: "Humility must always be the portion of any man who receives acclaim earned in the blood of his followers and the sacrifices of his friends."[6] Time and again, I heard veterans say, "I'm not the hero" as they recalled the names of the men who died at their side.

A heart filled with gratitude cannot be anything but humble.

Let me turn this illustration from the horizontal to the vertical. When I remember the suffering Christ endured on my behalf, how can I remain conceited for even a moment? When I appreciate that every breath I suck into my lungs is a gift from God, purchased by His Son's agony on the cross, how can I waste it on self-interest?

D. Martyn Lloyd-Jones wrote:

I am told that I am to esteem others better than myself, and there's only one thing that can make me do that—and thank God, it does make me do it—it is this. When I read the Bible I see the sinful nature that is in me; I see my failures, my shortcomings. But even then there is a tendency to defend them. There is only one thing I know of that crushes me to the ground, and humiliates me to the dust, and that is to look at the Son of God, and especially contemplate the cross.

> When I survey the wondrous cross
> On which the Prince of Glory died,
> My richest gain I count but loss,
> And pour contempt on all my pride.

Nothing else can do it. When I see that I am a sinner . . . that nothing but the Son of God on the cross can save me, I'm humbled to the dust . . . it is only the cross that makes me feel that. . . . Nothing but the cross can give us this spirit of humility. . . . It is only at the cross that this happens.[7]

Lloyd-Jones is absolutely correct. For the child of God the motivation for humility comes as a result of sustained reflection on Him who gave His blood for us in His sacrificial death on the cross.

HUMILITY AS AN ACT OF FAITH

Peter, like James and John, learned humility the hard way. As an expert on the subject, he knew that humility is an exercise in trust. He closed his letter to persecuted Christians with advice to their spiritual shepherds, urging them to avoid "lording over" God's people. They were instead to teach humility by example. Then he broadened his scope to include everyone, especially younger believers:

> All of you, clothe yourselves with humility toward one another, for God is opposed to the proud, but gives grace to the humble. Therefore humble yourselves under the mighty hand of God, that He may exalt you at the proper time, casting all your anxiety on Him, because He cares for you.
>
> —I PETER 5:5–7

I encourage you to pause here before reading on. Reread those words several times. Take a few moments to ponder what Peter wrote. He expressed four distinct thoughts, each of which could stand on its own. But he combined the four here for a reason. Why? Look at them one by one.

All of you, clothe yourselves with humility toward one another.

First, I find Peter's expression "clothe yourselves with humility" intriguing. The verb he used comes from a noun referring to a white scarf or apron typically worn by slaves. He may have been thinking of the last meal he had with Jesus when He taught His disciples a lesson in humility by example:

> [Jesus] got up from supper, and laid aside His garments; and taking a towel, He girded Himself. Then He poured water into the basin, and began to wash the disciples' feet and to wipe them with the towel with which He was girded.
>
> —JOHN 13:4–5

God is opposed to the proud, but gives grace to the humble.

Next, Peter quoted Proverbs 3:34 as he drove his second point home. The arrogant find themselves at odds with God, while the humble enjoy His blessings. Putting on humility as we relate to others enhances our relationship with God.

Humble yourselves under the mighty hand of God, that He may exalt you at the proper time.

The Greek phrase translated "humble yourselves under the mighty hand of God" is probably better rendered, "let yourselves be humbled under the mighty hand of God." In the Old Testament, the phrase "mighty hand of God" is used most often with two symbols in mind: God's hand of discipline and His hand of deliverance. Peter's third point? Submit to His discipline so you may receive His eventual blessing. Remember what we learned earlier? In God's kingdom plan, suffering brings reward.

Cast all your anxiety on Him, because He cares for you.

Of all the statements, this fourth one seems the most out of place. But here Peter addresses the core issue, the foundational problem to lack of humility, the source of self-interest: anxiety, the worry that if *we* don't watch out for ourselves, *nobody* will.

Humility—the discipline of putting others ahead of self, the choice to value others above self—is, at its core, a matter of faith. If we genuinely believe that "He cares for us," then we need never worry about serving our own interests. We can afford to focus our entire attention on meeting the needs of others because we have every confidence that God will spare nothing of His infinite resources to

Humility—the discipline of putting others ahead of self, the choice to value others above self—is, at its core, a matter of faith.

meet ours. In the meantime, allowing ourselves to be humbled by the mighty hand of God brings anxiety. It is here that the discipline of prayer will help. As Peter said, "cast all your anxiety on Him."

Don't worry if evil seems to be getting the upper hand as you humble yourself and obey God. He is Lord above all, including evil. Remember the story of Joseph? His hostile and brutal brothers originally plotted to kill him but sold him into slavery instead. He was falsely accused of groping his boss's wife and sentenced to an Egyptian prison, where he languished for at least two years, probably more. He was lonely, but he wasn't forgotten. At the proper time God exalted him. Joseph eventually became second-in-command to Pharaoh. When his brothers stood before him, knees knocking with fear, wondering if the brother they had wronged would use his power to exact his much-deserved revenge, they were surprised by what he had to say. He forgave them, treated them kindly, and gave them safety and provision.

Years later, his brothers still could not understand why Joseph had been so kind. His response revealed his humility: "You meant evil against me, but God meant it for good" (Genesis 50:20). Joseph understood what they did not. Humility, as with any act of faith, allows us to receive from God blessings that self-serving schemes can never match.

I like how Thomas à Kempis put it centuries ago. Paraphrasing, he said that it is the humble man whom God protects and liberates; it is the humble whom He loves and consoles. To the humble He turns and upon them bestows great grace, that after their humiliation He may raise them up to glory. He reveals His secrets to the humble, and with kind invitation bids them come to Him. Thus, the humble man enjoys peace in the midst of many vexations, because his trust is in God, not in the world.

SIT, STAND, BOW

In thinking of how to offer counsel on how to exercise the discipline of humility, I want you to imagine three postures. The first is from Mark 10, the second from Philippians 2, and the third from 1 Peter 5.

The story in Mark 10 teaches us: *we need to sit on promoting ourselves.* If we're really gifted, the people who want to use our talent will find us. If we're meant to be discovered and used in a significant way, God will bring it about, just as He did with Joseph. Sold into obscurity and doomed to rot in one of Egypt's deep, dark dungeons, God raised him to immense power in order to preserve Israel. Joseph's humility and integrity allowed God to have His way.

Sit on the temptation to promote yourself. Trust God to promote you when He determines that the time is appropriate. When He calls you, then rely on His calling and obey His Word.

Second, from Philippians 2 we learn: *we need to stand up for others.* We can encourage others to be humble by being sensitive to them in their needs. Look for opportunities to meet the needs of others, especially those whom many would consider the least deserving. (You know the one. He or she quite possibly popped into your mind as you read that last sentence.) Think of the least liked or most obnoxious person, or that person who has made a royal mess of life. Stand up for him or her. How can you become a servant to that person? Think of something simple that you can do soon. Don't put it off—do it. Then keep doing it.

Third, from 1 Peter 5 we learn: *we need to bow low before our God.* Accept His disciplines; don't resist them. Acknowledge His deliverances, which came from Him. Give Him all the praise and when you begin to feel anxious under the weight of His mighty hand, drop to your knees. Pray. Go back to the chapter on the discipline of prayer and release your care to Him. To be sure, the discipline of humility is an act of faith, and faith is never easy.

Douglas Southall Freeman ends his four-volume work on Robert E. Lee with a touching scene. General Lee was wrinkled and gray and stooped over—very close to death—when a young mother came to see him with her infant cradled in her arms. When Lee reached out for her baby, she responded by placing the infant in Lee's still-strong arms. The great general looked deeply into the child's eyes and then slowly turned to the mother and said, "Teach him he must deny himself."

The path to greatness in the kingdom of God will lead you through the valley of selflessness. Christlike humility will emerge on its own. Let it be. Let it be.

seven

Self-Control:

Holding Back

Never miss a good chance to shut up.

—WILL ROGERS

Self-Control:

Holding Back

Writing a book on spiritual disciplines is incredibly difficult. Not because the subject matter is boring, difficult to research, or hard to explain, but because it's so convicting. When you pick up a book, there is at least the implication that the author has mastered the subject. I can assure you that I have not! However, while perfection cannot be attained in this life, I can honestly say that I have improved . . . somewhat.

Many years ago I was sitting up late one night, relaxing in our family room and watching *SportsCenter*. The thought occurred to me, *That half-gallon of ice cream is just going to get old sitting over there in the freezer, and that would be a waste. I think I'll just have a few bites.* So I took the half-gallon container of Rocky Road out of the freezer (no need to dirty a clean dish!) and sat down with a spoon. I ate it all. In fact, I emptied it before *SportsCenter* was over. Are you ready? There's more. I microwaved the last part and drank the little bits that get caught around the seams of the container. Like I said, I hate wasting ice cream.

Suddenly, I realized that the kids were sure to notice that the ice cream was gone. They would never have noticed a missing ten-pound roast or half a turkey, but no one could get away with eating more than his fair share of ice cream. So I quietly sneaked out to my car, drove to the store, bought a new half-gallon—Rocky Road, of course—and carefully placed it right where the other one was. I was in the clear except for one tiny detail. I forgot that one of our kids had eaten a little bit out of the top of the other one. Busted! They let me know, in no uncertain terms, that they knew exactly what I had done. The whole family got in on that one.

THE UNIVERSAL CIVIL WAR

I've eaten too much, interfered where I had no business meddling, and spoken when I should have remained silent. Those are pretty common problems, aren't they? Universal, in fact. We have all exceeded the bounds of wisdom by failing to restrain ourselves. We all suffer from the same ailment: lack of self-control.

I would be a lot harder on myself were it not for Romans 7:14–25. I derive a lot of comfort from what the apostle Paul writes of his own experience. This man was an undisputed spiritual giant, called on by God to write God-breathed words and to lead thousands of believers on the journey to Christlikeness. Best of all, Paul led by example! He lived in submission to Christ no matter what. He was beaten, stoned, starved, shipwrecked, imprisoned, called a devil on one day and a god on another, and ultimately martyred for his faithfulness to the gospel. We might be tempted to think that he lived as close to perfection as the Lord Himself, were it not for his own admission.

Paul's candid confession in Romans 7 sounds exactly like yours or mine: "For what I am doing, I do not understand; for I am not practicing what I would like to do, but I am doing the very thing I hate" (Romans 7:15).

Look at that! The apostle Paul is openly declaring that he can't always follow the very commands he writes under inspiration. He's not saying that, theoretically, he sometimes behaves differently than he knows to be right. He's saying, "This is life as I live it. This is the unending struggle of life as I experience it. I don't understand this about myself. I decide one way and then I wind up acting another."

Check out what he said a little later. It gets worse: "For I know that nothing good dwells in me, that is, in my flesh; for the willing is present in me, but the doing of the good is not" (Romans 7:18).

I can will it, but I can't pull it off. I can want to do it right, but I can't make it happen.

How honest is that? Isn't that true for all of us? I can will it, but I can't pull it off. I can *want* to do right, but I can't make it happen. I promise myself at the beginning of the day, "I will not say what I shouldn't say." And then I ignore my better judgment and wind up saying it anyway, only to regret it and wish I could take it back. I can't count the times I have asked myself, "Why? Why did I do something so foolish?" Paul's analysis exposing the root cause comes back, loud and clear. I especially like Eugene Peterson's paraphrase:

> Something has gone wrong deep within me and gets the better of me every time.
>
> It happens so regularly that it's predictable. The moment I decide to do good, sin is there to trip me up. I truly delight in God's commands,

but it's pretty obvious that not all of me joins in that delight. Parts of me covertly rebel, and just when I least expect it, they take charge.

—ROMANS 7:20–23 MSG

Fritz Ridenour puts the inner struggle in different words in his fine book titled, *How to Be a Christian without Being Religious:*

What's your problem? Temper? Impatience? Self-control? Sex? Being honest? Your thought life? Pride? Laziness? Self-centeredness? Everyone has skeletons, and they don't always stay in the closet. You want to do right but you do wrong. You want to choose obedience but you choose sin. Sometimes you'd almost swear you were a split personality, a regular "walking civil war."[1]

We are in the middle of an inescapable fight, and I would suggest that most people fight it in the shadows, out of sight, and feeling all alone.

That's me. That's you. That's Paul. That's everyone. We're all in this "civil war" together! Can you admit it? Or do you try to convince everyone that you have some kind of consistent Spirit-walk going down the straight and narrow? Don't waste your time.

We are in the middle of an inescapable fight, and I would suggest that most people fight it in the shadows, out of sight, and feeling all alone. No wonder so many of us feel defeated by sin and seriously consider giving up. And when we are at our lowest, Satan slips his arm around our shoulders and whispers gently, *Face it: you'll never be good enough for those people—or for God. Why not just give up and accept the inevitable? And, besides, that thing you do doesn't really hurt anyone.* At that vulnerable moment, the enemy breaks through.

That reminds me of Proverbs 25:28: "Like a city that is broken into and without walls is a man who has no control over his spirit."

As we begin to address this universal problem, our inability to master the discipline of self-control, it is essential that we understand the consequences. Let me paraphrase Proverbs 25:28 in today's terms. *When we fail to control our desires—when we allow our natural inclinations to control us—we are like a bank vault with a screen door.* Failure to exercise the discipline of self-control is an open invitation for Satan to rob us of all the good things we receive from God.

KNOW YOUR ENEMY

Once we accept that everyone wages his or her own civil war and acknowledge the grave consequences of defeat, we are ready to begin our plan of attack with an honest assessment of the problem. Chinese general Sun Tzu wrote in *The Art of War,* "If you know the enemy and know yourself, you need not fear the results of a hundred battles."[2]

THE CYCLE OF SIN

According to Romans 7–8 and Galatians 5, the problem can be boiled down to one, five-letter word—*flesh:*

> The flesh sets its desire against the Spirit, and the Spirit against the flesh; for these are in opposition to one another, so that you may not do the things that you please. But if you are led by the Spirit, you are not under the Law. Now the deeds of the flesh are evident, which are: immorality, impurity, sensuality, idolatry, sorcery, enmities, strife,

jealousy, outbursts of anger, disputes, dissensions, factions, envying, drunkenness, carousing, and things like these, of which I forewarn you, just as I have forewarned you, that those who practice such things will not inherit the kingdom of God.

—GALATIANS 5:17–21

Because so many throughout history have misconstrued Paul's meaning of the word *flesh*, we must define it clearly and accurately. We cannot hope to win the war against this enemy if we don't understand the term as Paul intended.

If you truly are a believer in Jesus Christ, you have the Spirit of God dwelling within you.

If you truly are a believer in Jesus Christ, you have the Spirit of God dwelling within you. Yet believers also have an old nature—a habitual, sinful way of thinking—that Paul called "the flesh." Let me put it straight. The flesh is a self-serving, nonbelieving, godless mind-set that lives by animal instinct. Its natural stance is facing away from God. Its innate priority is self-preservation. The lens through which the flesh sees the world is "eat or be eaten." It's the pattern of living that you inherited when you were born, that the world taught you as you matured. To make matters worse, it comes as natural to you as breathing. The Holy Spirit notwithstanding, the flesh remains within us, never improving, always ready to be satisfied.

Many have mistaken Paul's meaning and have come to the conclusion that our physical body is innately evil. Some have even gone further, saying that our spirit—the nonmaterial part of our being—is good. This belief comes from the influence of ancient philosophy and is neither Christian nor biblical. In Genesis, God created the human body and called it good. But when Adam and Eve chose evil instead of obedience to God, they fell into sin completely—body and spirit, material and immaterial. Every part of their humanity became a slave to sin. So when Paul uses the word *flesh,* he doesn't refer only to the material, physical part of a person. He means the entire person's inclination in his or her former, before-Christ state—a condition that had them living in allegiance to the corrupted world, just like Adam and Eve after their fall into sin.

Here's how that influences our discussion. When you believed in Christ, your inner self was re-created. Everything changed for you, whether you were aware of it or not. But old habits die hard, and the flesh knows sin like you know how to ride a bicycle. It never forgets. Can you untrain your body so that you can no longer ride a bike? That's why the flesh can never conquer itself or choose not to sin when given a chance—and the world gives it numerous opportunities to ride again.

OUR FLESH VERSUS HIS SPIRIT

The flesh is most at home in the realm of wrong. I hardly need to remind you that we live in a world filled with twisted truth and distorted ethics. When you mix a flawed world with a failed nature, you've got the right combination for defeat.

On the other hand, if you are a believer in Jesus Christ, you also have the Spirit of God living in you. According to Galatians 5:16 the only hope we have against slavish obedience to the flesh is the Spirit. His re-creative work in us gives us the opportunity to let Him have His way instead. Paul writes, "But I say, walk by the Spirit, and you will not carry out the desire of the flesh."

What a profound statement! That's the foundation of living this thing we call the Christian life. The Spirit and our flesh are completely opposed to each other. While walking in the Spirit we cannot possibly carry out the desires of the flesh. So we're either operating from the realm of the Spirit and under His control, or we're operating in the realm of the flesh and under its control.

It's helpful to remember those things Paul identifies as "the deeds of the flesh." The following words describe those fleshly deeds in a way that captures the raw realities of sin:

> . . . repetitive, loveless, cheap sex; a stinking accumulation of mental and emotional garbage; frenzied and joyless grabs for happiness; trinket gods; magic-show religion; paranoid loneliness; cutthroat competition; all-consuming-yet-never-satisfied wants; a brutal temper; an impotence to love or be loved; divided homes and divided lives; small-minded and lopsided pursuits; the vicious habit of depersonalizing everyone into a rival; uncontrolled and uncontrollable addictions; ugly parodies of community. I could go on.
>
> —GALATIANS 5:19–21 MSG

Downright ugly, isn't it? What's worse is that the list is selective, not exhaustive. Face it, that's you and that's me. If the flesh wins too many battles in your own, personal civil war, then you become nothing more than a walking dead person. A generation ago we had a name for those who lived in that condition: carnal Christians. Flesh-driven believers.

Our bodies are a precious gift from God, so they are by no means evil. But given the opportunity, our bodily drives will rule us. Perhaps the most dangerous animals on the planet are believers who are so dominated by their flesh that they look no different than anyone else. Make no mistake: Christians are not immune to sin just because we have the Spirit of God living within us. Everything that tempted me as a lost person can defeat me now because I still have that same old nature. It doesn't improve. It never repents. The cutting remarks I used to make I can still make. I can still throw temper tantrums. Lustful thoughts can still invade my mind. I can still make these sins comfortable houseguests in my life. Therefore, in the power of the Spirit, I have to throw my hands up and say, "Get this stuff out of me. I can't conquer it!" As I confess my wrongdoing, He takes over, the battle is won, and I'm again walking in the light. What a difference He makes!

My teenage granddaughter, Heather, has a favorite CD by the contemporary Christian group DC Talk. While that music is not my particular cup of tea, the group ministers effectively to a different generation. The lyrics to DC Talk's song "In the Light," inspired by 1 John, describe the problem perfectly:

I keep trying to find a life
On my own, apart from you
I am the king of excuses
I've got one for every selfish thing I do

What's going on inside of me?
I despise my own behavior
This only serves to confirm my suspicions
That I'm still a man in need of a saviour

I wanna be in the Light
As You are in the Light
I wanna shine like the stars in the heavens
Oh, Lord be my Light and be my Salvation

'Cause all I want is to be in the Light
All I want is to be in the Light[3]

THE GOOD NEWS

If I ended the chapter with our battle with the flesh, we'd be in a heap of trouble. Fortunately God has followed up this bad news with some very good news. God is personally at work in all of His people. He's given us the power and the presence of His Holy Spirit. As corrupting as sin has been, His Spirit is all the more cleansing. Where the flesh leads only to a foul harvest of sin, the Spirit produces an abundance of sweet fruit:

> But the fruit of the Spirit is love, joy, peace, patience, kindness, goodness, faithfulness, gentleness, self-control; against such things there is no law.
>
> —GALATIANS 5:22–23

Talk about an attractive list! Go back and read again those nine qualities the Spirit of God produces within us. When the Holy Spirit takes up residence in the believer, these are what He begins to produce in us and through us. I'm sure that this list of nine qualities, like the other list of the "deeds of the flesh," isn't exhaustive but selective. Take note of the last quality Paul named: self-control.

SELF-CONTROL LEADS TO GREATER FREEDOM

As we cultivate the discipline of self-control, you and I can experience victory over the very things we despise in ourselves. The new nature trumps the old nature as we allow the Spirit of God to rule our minds and our hearts. As He does His transforming work, we will find that when the flesh runs to do evil, He will shout, "Stop! Don't go any further. Don't go there. Don't say that. Think of the consequences." As a result, life soon begins to improve because the restraining power of the Holy Spirit overcomes the tempting urges of the flesh. He brings strength we do not have in ourselves.

Enkrateia is the Greek word translated "self-control." The stem is the term *kratos,* meaning strength or might. Often *kratos* is translated "dominion." The prefix personalizes the word, in a manner of speaking. So *enkrateia* is the ability to have dominion over one's impulses or desires.

The exercise of this discipline called self-control prevents desire from becoming dictator. For the person without Christ, the desires dictate and he or she obeys. Those in Christ, living under the authority of His Spirit and ruled by Him, are able to defy this once-powerful dictator. As a result, we experience a transforming change that others notice.

The exercise of this discipline called self-control prevents desire from becoming dictator.

As for the tongue, we exercise verbal restraint. Where our diet is concerned, we exercise restraint at the dinner table. (And I leave the ice cream in the freezer!) Pertaining to the temper, we exercise emotional restraint. As it relates to our thoughts, we exercise mental restraint. In terms of sexual lust, we exercise moral restraint. All of us have areas that tempt us more than others, so we must give ourselves over to the Spirit's authority. He steps in and empowers us to hold back before we take steps to satisfy our impulse or our desire.

Let's get practical. I have found that a three-second pause can make all the difference. Just as an impulse hits me, I decide to wait just three seconds before taking any action. During that pause, I do a quick assessment of what the consequences might be. Would this action be something that I would be embarrassed about later? Not all impulses are bad; some are good. Those three seconds have kept me out of a lot of hot water over the years.

Sometimes I know that I shouldn't act, so I pray, "Right now, Lord, in this very moment, I'm struggling. Spirit of God, control my tongue. Stop my mind from dwelling on that thought. Don't let that impulse have its way." Obviously all of that happens in an instant, and I rarely say those words out loud. But I am frequently amazed by how effectively the Lord provides self-control when I need it. As I release the struggle to Him, He takes over. Every time.

This mastery of self is an incredibly difficult discipline, but it's the path to freedom. Maxie Dunham put it well:

> The purpose of self-control is that we may be fit for God, fit for ourselves, and fit to be servants of others. . . . It is not a rigid, religious practice—discipline for discipline's sake. It is not dull drudgery aimed at exterminating laughter and joy. It is the doorway to true joy, true liberation from the stifling slavery of self-interest and fear.[4]

WINNING THE WAR

Now that we know the enemy, what can we do to defeat it? If we are to win, self-control plays a major role in the victory. We read Paul's candid confession earlier as he described his private "civil war" between the flesh and the Spirit. Let's observe another admission Paul makes. With intensity, he writes of the importance of discipline:

> Do you not know that those who run in a race all run, but only one receives the prize? Run in such a way that you may win. Everyone who competes in the games *exercises self-control* in all things. They

then do it to receive a perishable wreath, but we an imperishable. Therefore I run in such a way, as not without aim; I box in such a way, as not beating the air; but *I discipline my body and make it my slave,* so that, after I have preached to others, I myself will not be disqualified.

—I CORINTHIANS 9:24–27, emphasis added

RUN WITH PURPOSE AND HAVE A STRATEGY

Like many Corinthian citizens, Paul was a sports fan. He often inserted athletic terms in his writings. Here is a case in point. The Isthmian Games, held every two years near Corinth, were almost as popular as the Olympic Games. Competitions included running, wrestling, and boxing, from which Paul drew this particular set of word pictures. Using images familiar to every Corinthian would help him establish the link between discipline and excellence.

The Isthmian Games were open to anyone who wanted to enter, and, as with any race, all those who entered would run. Obviously, the object of running the race is to be the first person across the tape . . . to win! It's not just a matter of putting on spikes, wearing the outfit, and enjoying the scenery. Don't merely run, but, as Paul puts it, "Run in such a way that you may win." Paul's hope is that we will run with purpose. He desires for all of us to become winners, not merely runners.

So, what's the secret? How do winners compete? "Everyone who competes in the games exercises self-control in all things" (v. 25). It's always required the same secret: discipline. Those who run to win exercise restraint over their impulses and emotions and desires. Olympic hopefuls are this very day watching their diet, getting sufficient sleep, and training their bodies in just the right way for just the right amount of time. They are not fudging on anything that might hedge their performance on the track, on the bike, in the pool, or in the ring. And they measure the consequences of every impulse to judge whether it will assist them or hinder them from fulfilling the purpose of competition: winning the gold.

Paul mentions "a perishable wreath." The Isthmian Games were centuries old, starting with the Greeks and carried on by the Romans. By the first century the prize was a crown made of woven pine fronds in honor of Poseidon, god of the sea. But that's not all. Victors were treated like royalty both at the games and in their hometowns. Officials would break a large opening in the city wall and fill it with a brass covering bearing the engraved name of the winner. His debts were canceled, and he was allowed to live tax-free for the rest of his life. Sometimes he would be given a lifetime supply of food, so that he could literally rest on his laurels.

But stop and think: as impressive and enjoyable as those rewards were, they were all temporary, all perishable—the brass will tarnish, the wreath will wither, the fame will fade. And at the end of life, temporal comforts will mean nothing. Paul pointed out that, as valuable as the leafy crown was for the moment, it cannot compare to the eternal rewards for which we strive. We run a race called life for a prize of unimaginable worth, and to win it we must exercise the discipline of restraint—self-control.

Look carefully at Paul's personal testimony: "Therefore I run in such a way, as not without aim; I box in such a way, as not beating the air" (v. 26). He says, in effect, "My focus is Christ. Christ only, Christ alone. He's the goal *and* the prize for which I run. And I'm not shadow boxing. I have a very real opponent; I battle the adversary."

SHOW YOUR BODY WHO'S BOSS

I love how down to earth Paul gets with his next word picture: "I discipline my body and make it my slave" (v. 27). The Greek word translated "discipline" here literally means "to strike under the eye." It is the word for beating the face black and blue. But that's not to say we're to abuse our bodies for the sake of discipline. Some people take that to extremes, literally and repeatedly punching their bodies as a means of keeping themselves under control. Even in Paul's day the word was a figure of speech. It was one of those humorous, extreme word pictures we sometimes use to describe our actions. My granddaughter is a runner. She might say, "Bubba, I'm gonna have to kill myself to get ready for that cross-country meet."

The purpose of this discipline over the body is, as the literal Greek would put it, "to enslave it." Like an athlete, we have to show our bodies who's boss. That includes saying no to its whining wish that we indulge its every whim. The point of disciplined self-control is to make the body serve us rather than the other way around. That makes all the sense in the world if you've ever encountered an addict. His body cries out for a

Like an athlete, we have to show our bodies who's boss.

substance that is so satisfying its craving becomes goal number one. Every thought, every decision, every action, every motivation becomes the tool of his body's desires. He or she is enslaved to it. Paul not only demanded that we exercise the discipline of self-control; he also modeled it.

I read an article about a young basketball prodigy named Dwight Howard in the June 21, 2004, issue of *Sports Illustrated.* He's six feet ten, 240 pounds, and one of an elite group of athletes who is qualified to play basketball at the professional level right out of high school. Dwight's dad said, "We have come to realize that our three kids are a living testament to the grace and wisdom of God, and that God allowed them to be here to worship and glorify Him." (How's that for the goal of a dad?)

God will do His part, but there is a part that we play, both in terms of long-term, disciplined preparation and those immediate three second pauses where we invite the Lord to take control of the moment.

Dwight was chosen to join other national all-star players in an event called the Capital Classic. Michael Jordan addressed the group and then opened the floor for questions. The first to lift his hand was high schooler Dwight Howard, who wanted to know about the sacrifices that champions must make. Michael Jordan said, "When other players are sleeping, that's when you want to be out there working. . . . Work hard. Be the best. Demand a lot from yourself, then when you earn that respect, be demanding of others."

That's exactly what Paul did with the church in Corinth and what he does for us by way of Scripture. Having earned our respect from his own testimony—"I run, I box, I discipline my body, keeping it under control"—he then demands the same from us. "You run in such a way that you may win." God will do His part, but there is a part that we play, both in terms of long-term, disciplined preparation and those immediate three-second pauses where we invite the Lord to take control of the moment instead of yielding to a wayward impulse.

MEETING OUR IMPULSES HEAD-ON

I need to clarify the difference between temptation and indulgence. Not every stray thought, no matter how graphic or angry or ugly it may be, makes you guilty. And let's face it: we live in a world where sensual images constantly assault us from the least likely places.

A couple of years ago I was on an annual retreat with our church leader. After a busy afternoon of work, most of us men decided to relax and watch a championship playoff game between the Lakers and the Pistons. The Lakers weren't playing very well, so the network kept switching back and forth from the game to coach Phil Jackson. As the gap in the score widened, he was getting more and more perturbed.

Just over Phil Jackson's shoulder was a woman wearing a low-cut blouse and, well . . . let's just say she filled it to overflowing. There was more of her than blouse. Whenever the cameraman showed the coach, he made sure to frame the shot to include the woman. Not her face, mind you. Just what he, and most red-blooded men in America, would find most interesting. Not surprisingly the network showed the coach *a lot* during the latter part of the game. With each shot of Jackson, we saw less of the coach and more of the sports fan behind him—though never her face.

I noticed that the pastors grew more and more silent, and after a little while it was as quiet as a room full of nuns. Finally I blurted out, "Kinda hard to keep looking at Phil Jackson, isn't it?" The guys burst into laughter, and every ounce of tension fled away. I don't think anyone there was guilty of lust, though that's exactly how it can start. In an unguarded, unexpected moment, something grabs our attention, and without appropriate boundaries and an honest acknowledgement of the temptation, we can yield. We can dwell on the image, nurture it into a fantasy, and even in the middle of a room full of pastors, allow the impulse to drag us into lust. But simply noticing an enticing image doesn't qualify as a lack of self-control. What happens in the next five seconds may or may not, depending on what we choose to do.

Paul obviously had the same penchant for lack of self-control as the rest of us. He says, "I discipline my body and make it my slave, so that, after I have preached to others, I myself will not be disqualified" (v. 27). I wish that full-time ministry made the battle against the flesh easier, but it doesn't. And even when a man is writing God-breathed words, he still has to suit up and face the enemy in a civil war that never skips a day.

FIRST STEPS TO LIVING ABOVE THE FLESH

Now, if we can't win this fight, then Scripture is mocking us by dangling a hope that will never be realized. And to put it bluntly, Paul is a liar. But fortunately, we're in a winnable war. Paul isn't lying. Our study of these passages leads to four truths, four perspectives that will arm us for the conflict.

First, *appreciating the nature of the battle is essential.* It's a universal war that began all the way back in the Garden of Eden and includes every one of us. Our flesh craves satisfaction in the very things that God hates. And until we stand with the Savior in heaven, the age-old civil war rages on! Yes, we will experience the attack of Satan from the outside, but we have an enemy within that we must never forget. The flesh never takes a holiday.

Second, *we are powerless to win the war against the flesh without the Spirit of God.* By conscious submission, we engage the Holy Spirit in the first moments of each decision. Our ability to do that will grow as we continue practicing the spiritual disciplines. All of them prepare us for battle. All of them give us greater intimacy with the Almighty, who lives within us. The result is predictable: when faced with temptation, He fights the battle on our behalf.

Third, *developing this discipline is a personal matter.* We can depend upon no one else to develop our own discipline of self-control. Paul says, "*I* box, *I* run, *I* discipline *my* body." This is something only we can do in the Lord's strength. If someone else has to restrain us, it's not *self*-control!

As a pastor, I've seen a lot of people marry with the hope that his or her partner's strength will prop up their own weakness. The opposite is more often the case. Marriage isn't a magic pill. A godly marriage can be the instrument of God's working to make us more holy, but marriage by itself makes nobody strong. Developing the discipline of self-control cannot be the responsibility of a husband or wife.

Fourth, *ignoring the consequences invites disaster.* Lack of self-control will invariably lead to embarrassment for us and those we love. With issues of self-control, we're usually dealing with things that we know are wrong or will have negative fallout. And they usually involve something habitual, which means that the people we hurt are probably growing weary. What's worse, it negatively affects our spiritual life.

In verse 27, Paul uses a word that most translations render "disqualified." It's in keeping with the word picture of the athletic competition, but "disqualified" can lead us to some wrong conclusions about the spiritual consequences. Salvation and the assurance of heaven are not the issues in Paul's mind here. You will not lose your salvation if you fail to control yourself. However, you quite possibly can be put out of the race by God's disciplinary action. I have seen, on more than one occasion, a believer sidelined by God for the good of the family, the church, and the individual.

The word that Paul uses can also mean "worthless, of no account, useless," or in the context of a race, a last-place loser. We're in the race called life, and God calls us to run it with purpose, to restrain our impulses so as not to be too flabby to run well. And His desire is that we enjoy victory and not have to go through life labeled a loser because we defeated ourselves.

In the chapter on the discipline of surrender, I referred to Hebrews 12:1–2, which pictures a stadium filled with faithful saints who cheer us on in this footrace we call life. The author of that book encourages us to study the example of Christ then use His techniques, run in His footsteps, and emulate His running style so that we may enjoy the spoils of victory. There is no greater example of self-control than Jesus. Richard J. Foster presents an airtight case:

> Have you ever noticed the number of times Jesus refused to use power? He refused to dazzle people by jumping off the pinnacle of the temple (Matthew 4:5). He rejected the temptation to make more "wonder bread" to validate His ministry (John 6:26). He refused to do many wonderful works in His own hometown because of the unbelief of the people (Luke 4:16–27). He said no to the Pharisees when they demanded He give a sign to prove He was the Messiah (Matthew 12:38). At His arrest, Jesus said He could have summoned a whole army of angels but He did not (Matthew 26:53).[5]

You want to be like Christ? Refuse to surrender to the flesh, surrender instead to the Spirit, and let Him live His life through you.

eight

Sacrifice:

Giving Over

He is no fool who gives what he cannot keep
to gain what he cannot lose.

—JIM ELLIOT

Sacrifice:

Giving Over

If the disciplines form a small mound of gems, then sacrifice is the diamond at the top. No other discipline is more closely associated with the character and the mission of Jesus Christ than sacrifice. Yes, He was intimate with the Father, lived simply, sought solitude, surrendered His will to the Father daily, and lived a prayerful, humble life characterized by self-control. But it is sacrifice that distinguishes the Son of God from all mere historical figures and identifies Him as Savior—even to those who scarcely know of Him.

As we return to our key verse to reestablish the goal in our minds, notice again the extent to which Paul says he wants to be transformed into His likeness:

[For my determined purpose is] that I may know Him—that I may progressively become more deeply and intimately acquainted with Him, perceiving and recognizing and understanding [the wonders of His Person] more strongly and more clearly, and that I may in that same way come to know the power outflowing from His resurrection [which it exerts over believers]; and that I may so share His sufferings as to be continually transformed [in spirit into His likeness even] to His death.

—PHILIPPIANS 3:10 AMP

Did you catch it: "to be continually transformed even to His death"? You want to be like Christ? Become a person characterized by the discipline of sacrifice—the ultimate expression of Christlikeness.

BECOME A LIVING, BREATHING SACRIFICE

But what does that involve? What *is* sacrifice? The term is so old and so strange to our ears it's like an ancient relic from a forgotten age. And I will admit to you that I was a fully grown man—married, in fact—before I understood the first thing about it. I told you a little about how God interrupted my idyllic life in order to draw me closer to Him, how He commandeered the life plan I had carefully arranged so that I would cultivate a deeper intimacy with Him. Let me share the details of that story and what I learned about the discipline of sacrifice in the forty-five-plus years since that time.

During my final weekend in early January 1958, I was in a Marine staging regiment back at Camp Pendleton, preparing to ship out. I had a negative attitude toward life in general and toward God in particular. To be honest, I was borderline bitter. Why on earth would He have allowed this to happen? I was convinced I would never smile again.

Rather than hang out in the barracks that final weekend in the States, I decided to take a bus to Pasadena to visit my older brother, Orville, and his wife, Erma Jean. Our time together sped by quickly, and soon I needed to catch the bus back to Camp Pendleton. Just before my brother said good-bye, he handed me a book and told me,

"You'll never be the same after you read this." I had no intention of even opening it. I shrugged and mumbled an insincere, "Thanks," as I got on the bus. It was a rainy, cold night. I blinked through tears of loneliness and self-pity as I sat staring out the window. I couldn't even pray. A hard rain hammered against the oversized bus window. My world had collapsed.

Then for some unexplainable reason, I decided to dig into my bag and pull out the book Orville had given me. I flipped on the tiny light above my head as my eyes gazed across the title: *Through Gates of Splendor.* I thought I recognized those words as being from one of the hymns I had sung in church. I opened the book and soon discovered that it was the true account of how five young men had been murdered—really, martyred—by a small tribe of Auca Indians in the Ecuadorian jungle.

The painfully raw and realistic pictures in the book held my attention. One was a tragic scene: the body of one of the missionaries, speared to death and left floating downriver. That did it! I was hooked. I decided that maybe it wouldn't hurt to glance over a chapter or two, if for no other reason than to get my mind off myself.

Seven hours later I finished the last page. I was on the floor back at the barracks, sitting under the only light that stayed on all night. It was just before dawn. I can remember as if it were yesterday. All alone, I laid the book aside, put my head in my hands and sobbed audibly. Sitting there on that concrete floor, I realized I had just spent all night enraptured by the story of five brave young men whose hearts beat for Christ. Their passion was to win the hearts of that tribe of Aucas for the singular purpose of introducing each one of them to the Lord Jesus, who had died for their sins. Their ultimate hope in life was not self-centered. On the contrary, it was Christ-centered. Here were five young men fairly near my own age, whose passion for Him was intense—driven by the hope that those in that dangerous tribe might come to know and love Jesus and thereby gain the assurance of forgiveness, secure their eternal life in heaven, and discover His transforming power.

I found myself rebuked. There I was, preoccupied by self-pity because things hadn't gone as I had expected. And here were a few men who sacrificed their entire lives for a cause that made my situation pale into insignificance. The contrast was embarrassingly real! As one of the men had written so eloquently in his personal journal, "He is no fool who gives what he cannot keep to gain what he cannot lose."

I realized that life doesn't revolve around me . . . Clearly, it is all about Him.

I cannot describe the change that swept over me as I watched the morning sun break through the windows. My depression had slowly lifted during that night—it never returned. Beginning that morning and throughout the seventeen days aboard the troopship across the Pacific, my whole attitude toward life began a transformation. God used this example of selflessness—the sacrifice of those men—to teach me the value of caring more about others than myself. He taught me so many lessons regarding trusting instead of fearing and worrying, seeing His hand at work in difficulties instead of always asking why. I realized that *life doesn't revolve around me*—*my* comfort, *my* desires, *my* dreams, *my* plans. Clearly, it is *all about Him.* I became a changed man. In the months that followed, that change in perspective made all the difference in how I viewed life. It still does!

Candidly, I am convinced I am in the Lord's work today because I read Elisabeth Elliot's book on the darkest night of my life up to that point. God used her words to touch my soul and reach my heart with His calling to ministry, a vocation fueled by the discipline of sacrifice.

God will occasionally ask some of His own to suffer death for the sake of Christ, but that is not the sacrifice He wants from most of us. He desires that we offer ourselves as nothing less than living sacrifices. You read that correctly. Each one of us is called to become a "living sacrifice."

Those are the words Paul used in his letter to his Christian friends in Rome. In Romans 12:1 (NLT), we find Paul on his knees before us, begging, "I plead with you." Why beg? Because what he's asking for doesn't come naturally or easily or automatically. When people sacrifice, they're usually not doing it on a whim. Sacrifice hurts. Sacrifice works against our natural inclinations to keep a tight hold on our possessions and creature comforts. And we come hard-wired with the instinct to watch out for ourselves, guard against risk, and preserve our own lives at any cost.

The dictionary would call the phrase *living sacrifice* an oxymoron, a term that is logically self-defeating. Paul's odd expression is a lot like telling someone to become a living martyr. How can that be? To become a martyr, one has to die. In this case Paul isn't asking us to seek our own demise, not literally. He is, however, pleading for us to give up our life as we continue living it. When we get out of bed in the morning, as we arrive at work and put in those hours, as we relate, as we play, as we carry out our personal responsibilities then fall into bed for the night, we are to do everything as a deliberate act of submission out of obedience to God. That path leads to our becoming a living, breathing sacrifice—dead to anything our Master hates, devoted to everything He loves.

The word Paul uses in Romans 12:1, rendered "sacrifice," is the Greek term *thysia*. Interestingly he uses it sparingly, just a handful of times in all of his letters. That says to me that it was not a term he tossed around loosely or lightly, so we should sit up and pay attention whenever we see it. *Thysia* is the same word we find in the book of Hebrews, referring to the Old Testament temple sacrifices, looking toward what Jesus would one day do on the cross.

In Ephesians 5:1–2, Paul calls for us to be like Christ, and he defines the kind of sacrifice we are to make of ourselves: "Therefore be imitators of God, as beloved children; and walk in love, just as Christ also loved you and gave Himself up for us, an offering and a sacrifice to God as a fragrant aroma."

To sacrifice is to give up something for the sake of something else that is much better.

In that sentence, two significant ideas are placed side by side: offering and sacrifice, *prosphora* and *thysia*. Both picture someone giving up something. In each case the giver no longer has something that is valuable in his possession. But there is a slight distinction, a subtle difference that makes all the difference. An offering is a sacrifice with an added element: choice. To sacrifice is to give up something for the sake of something else that is much better. An offering is a voluntary act. Christ made a conscious choice to offer Himself as an atoning sacrifice so that He might have us. We are to make that same choice for the sake of having Him in a more intimate way. Not to earn His pleasure or blessing, but as a means of deeply coming to know Him.

As with all of the disciplines, the exercise of sacrifice begins small. As we consistently carry it out, it becomes habitual. To cultivate the discipline of sacrifice, we must apply it in at least three realms of our lives: personal, relational, and material.

PERSONAL SACRIFICE

In Matthew 6, we find a record of the day when Jesus delivered His Sermon on the Mount to His friends and followers. He came on rather strong when He started to discuss material wealth and things that have price tags. (It's good to remember that everything costs something.) As you read His words to them, you will not see the term *sacrifice*. Keep the word in the back of your mind, however, as you read.

Do not store up for yourselves treasures on earth, where moth and rust destroy, and where thieves break in and steal. But store up for yourselves treasures in heaven, where neither moth nor rust destroys, and where thieves do not break in or steal; for where your treasure is, there your heart will be also.

The eye is the lamp of the body; so then if your eye is clear, your whole body will be full of light. But if your eye is bad, your whole body will be full of darkness. If then the light that is in you is darkness, how great is the darkness!

No one can serve two masters; for either he will hate the one and love the other, or he will be devoted to one and despise the other. You cannot serve God and wealth.

For this reason I say to you, do not be worried about your life, as to what you will eat or what you will drink; nor for your body, as to what you will put on. Is not life more than food, and the body more than clothing? Look at the birds of the air, that they do not sow, nor reap nor gather into barns, and yet your heavenly Father feeds them. Are you not worth much more than they? And who of you by being worried can add a single hour to his life? And why are you worried about clothing? Observe how the lilies of the field grow; they do not toil nor do they spin, yet I say to you that not even Solomon in all his glory clothed himself like one of these. But if God so clothes the grass of the field, which is alive today and tomorrow is thrown into the furnace, will He not much more clothe you? You of little faith! Do not worry then, saying, "What will we eat?" or "What will we drink?" or "What will we wear for clothing?" For the Gentiles eagerly seek all these things; for your heavenly Father knows that you need all these things. But seek first His kingdom and His righteousness, and all these things will be added to you.

—MATTHEW 6:19–33

I find at least two sermons in Jesus's words. The first one is on hoarding—the greedy grappling for more and more stuff. Complicating life with better, larger, more expensive, more extravagant things that bind us to mandatory service to maintain them. Anytime you hear a sermon on this passage, that's what the preacher usually goes for. It's a valid focus, and I will be addressing financial sacrifice later. However, any sermon based on Jesus's words that only condemns materialism is but half a sermon.

Being the master communicator, Jesus used word pictures that even a little child could understand. A little moth that can eat a garment. A bit of rust that can ultimately destroy a piece of steel. I love His sense of humor drawn from a scene in nature: "Look up in the air. Look at those birds. They don't sow. They don't reap. They don't store food in barns" (see v. 26).

From what I've observed, they spend all their time in the parking lot at McDonald's. That's where the food is! And I've never seen one of them shake his head and say, "Man, I'm so worried about where that next French fry is going to come from. I mean . . . what if somebody doesn't drop his Coke this evening?" Jesus assured His listeners that our heavenly Father cares about them. He went on to point out that if He takes care of birds and flowers, certainly He will attend to our needs.

Personal sacrifice begins with a choice: who will we trust to meet our needs? We naturally serve what we trust. Hoarding wealth is a sure sign that a person trusts his things instead of his God.

I mentioned my older brother, Orville, at the beginning of this chapter. He was a missionary for more than thirty years in Buenos Aires. Just before that, he had done some short-term mission work in Mexico and had come north to gather his wife, Erma Jean, and the kids for the long trip down into the heart of South America.

Before leaving, they stopped off for a quick visit with our parents. Now, you have to appreciate the kind of man my father was. Look up the word *responsible* in the dictionary, and his picture is there! To him, risks are for those who fail to plan. Responsible people leave nothing to chance. As far as he was concerned, faith is something you exercise when your three backup plans fall through and you have run out of all other options. My father was a believer, but he never understood the life of faith. Not really.

My brother, on the other hand, was stimulated by faith. He has lived his entire adult life on the raw edge of faith. To him, life doesn't get exciting until only God can get us through some specific challenge. That drove Dad nuts!

Orville pulled up to the house in an old Chevy on four of the slickest tires I had ever seen. My father always inspected tires when we came to visit, and he occasionally even checked the tank to see if we had enough gas. I wondered how long it would take for him to say something. I'm sure Orville did too. Not very, is the answer.

After a great supper of good ol' collard greens and cornbread, onions, and red beans, my mother and sister went into the kitchen, leaving my father at one end of the table, Orville at the other, and me sitting on one side. Then it started.

"Son, how much money do you have for your long trip?"

"Oh, Dad, don't worry about it. We're gonna be fine."

Before he could change the subject, my father pressed the issue. "Son, how much money do you have in your wallet?"

Orville smiled as he said, "I don't have any money in my wallet."

I sat silent, watching this verbal tennis match.

"How much money do you have? You're gettin' ready to go down to South America! How much money you got?"

With that, my brother dug into his pocket, pulled out a quarter, set it on its edge on his end of the table, then gave it a careful thump. It slowly rolled past me all the way to my father's end of the table and fell into his hand. Dad said, "That is all you've got?"

Orville broke into an even bigger smile and said, "Yeah. *Isn't that exciting!*"

That was not the word my father had in mind at the moment. After a heavy sigh and a very brief pause, Dad shook his head and said, "Orville, I just don't understand you."

My brother grew serious. Looking Dad in the eyes, he answered, "No, Dad, you never have."

I don't know how he actually made the trip or how he and Erma Jean took care of all their little kids, but they never went hungry. And they served in Buenos Aires and other parts of South America for more than three decades. My father was a man who emerged through the Great Depression, lived in fear of poverty his whole life, and never experienced the joy of trusting God, regardless, that made my brother smile so big that day.

The point of Jesus's sermon was not to say that having nice things is wrong. Read the passage again and look for anything that would suggest that He wanted people to be poor.

As I said in the chapter on prayer, He may want some to be poor as the disciples and He were. Yet He may want others to have an overabundance of money and material goods that they might give in abundance. His point is not about wealth; it's about us. Whether or not we own nice things, He wants to be sure that we aren't owned by them! As soon as something begins to feel just a little too crucial to our happiness or safety, it's time to apply the discipline of sacrifice.

Are you open to a little advice for no extra charge? Show your material stuff who's boss by giving it away.

Richard Foster tells this story on himself.

Not long ago we had a swing set, not one of those store-bought aluminum things but a real custom-made job—huge steel pipes and all. But our children would soon be beyond swing sets, so we decided it would be good to sell it at a garage sale. My next decision was what price to put on it. I went out in the backyard and looked it over. "It should bring a good price," I thought to myself. "In fact if I touched up the paint just a bit I could ante it up some, and if I fixed the seat on the glider I could charge even more. . . ."

All of a sudden I began to monitor a spirit of covetousness within me, and I became aware of how really dangerous it was spiritually. Well, I went into the house and rather tentatively asked my wife, Carolyn, if she would mind if we gave the swing set away rather than selling it.

"No, not at all!" she responded quickly. I thought to myself, "Rats!" But before the day was out we had found a couple with young children who could make good use of it, and we gave it to them—and I didn't even have to paint it! The simple act of giving crucified the greed that had gripped my heart, and the power of money was broken—for the time being.[1]

May I press the point? When was the last time you just gave something away? I mean something very nice. Something that has meant something to you. It won't be easy. Sacrifice doesn't come naturally. It's a discipline that requires faith—a trust that the Almighty will look after your needs in ways that you will never see until you allow Him the opportunity.

Dallas Willard explains it much better than I:

> The discipline of sacrifice is one in which we forsake the security of meeting our needs with what is in our hands. It is total abandonment to God, a stepping into the darkened abyss in the faith and hope that God will bear us up. . . .
>
> The cautious faith that never saws off a limb on which it is sitting never learns that unattached limbs may find strange, unaccountable ways of not falling.[2]

I wonder how much better we would know our God if we didn't make such a good living. I would be willing to wager that we don't have intimacy with the Almighty because we haven't given enough away. We don't really trust our God sufficiently. To exercise the spiritual discipline of sacrifice start cultivating generosity.

RELATIONAL SACRIFICE

Genesis 22 tells a story of Abraham's triumph over unbelief. Abraham and Sarah had waited their entire marriage to have their own child. God had promised them a son decades before, but it wasn't until Abraham was one hundred and Sarah was ninety that Isaac came along. (Pause and imagine what you just read.) But that little lad was more than just an addition to the household; he was the son of promise. God had told Abraham that he would be the father of a great nation, a people who would inhabit the land of promise and worship the one true God. All of God's promises to Abraham rested in this one son. How easy for Isaac to become virtually *everything* to his father! One evening the Lord stepped into Abraham's world: "Take now your son, your only son, whom you love, Isaac, and go to the land of Moriah, and offer him there as a burnt offering on one of the mountains of which I will tell you" (Genesis 22:2).

I'm convinced that Abraham spent a restless night, if not in anguish, at least in soul-searching prayer. Let's face it, Abraham was a hero of faith, but we dare not turn him into a superhero. He was just a man. Imagine how you would feel if you were asked to take the life of your child. Just like you or me, Abraham had to evaluate his priorities and check his faith. After all, God didn't stutter. His voice was clear. He had unmistakable orders from the Lord: "Sacrifice your son."

While I'm sure Abraham didn't sleep at all that night, we are told that he wasted no time obeying:

> So Abraham rose early in the morning and saddled his donkey, and took two of his young men with him and Isaac his son; and he split wood for the burnt offering, and arose and went to the place of which God had told him. On the third day Abraham raised his eyes and saw the place from a distance. Abraham said to his young men, "Stay here with the donkey, and I and the lad will go over there; and we will worship and return to you."
>
> —GENESIS 22:3–5

Don't hurry past how Abraham explained his plan to his servants. "We will go." And then? "We will worship." What a great perspective! Sacrifice is worship. Notice also, *"and* return to you." In the Hebrew, Abraham was specific in his use of the plural. He didn't say, *"We* will go worship, and *I* will return to you." We cannot know for sure what he was thinking. He knew that he would have to kill Isaac, but he also knew that God would keep His promises—the promises that rest in Isaac. Hebrews 11:17–19 clearly states that Abraham knew God could raise Isaac from the dead once he sacrificed his life on the altar. Whatever his thinking, he obeyed:

> Abraham took the wood of the burnt offering and laid it on Isaac his son, and he took in his hand the fire and the knife. So the two of them walked on together. Isaac spoke to Abraham his father and said, "My father!" And he said, "Here I am, my son." And he said, "Behold, the fire and the wood, but where is the lamb for the burnt offering?"
>
> —GENESIS 22:6–7

Isaac had been mentored in the sacrifices. He had helped his father prepare sacrifices before. He saw the torch and the firewood, but saw no animal. Abraham was so wise. Now he mentors his son in faith:

> Abraham said, "God will provide for Himself the lamb for the burnt offering, my son." So the two of them walked on together.
>
> —GENESIS 22:8

The whole story turns on trust. There's no argument, there's no further questioning, and the boy trusts his dad. Even better, the dad is confident in his God:

> Then they came to the place of which God had told him; and Abraham built the altar there and arranged the wood, and bound his son Isaac and laid him on the altar, on top of the wood. Abraham stretched out his hand and took the knife to slay his son. But the angel of the LORD called to him from heaven and said, "Abraham,

Abraham!" And he said, "Here I am." He said, "Do not stretch out your hand against the lad, and do nothing to him; for now I know that you fear God, since you have not withheld your son, your only son, from Me."

—GENESIS 22:9–12

God took Abraham all the way to the edge of his relationship with his son. This faithful servant said by his actions, "Lord, You're more to me than any relationship ever will be. If You tell me to put the most important person in the world to me on an altar, I'll sacrifice him."

Unlike my brother, when Abraham rolled his quarter across the table, as it were, it landed in the hands of One who fully understood—and even rewarded—his act of faith.

You may have someone who means a great deal to you, whom you have to give up. God asked Abraham to lay his son on a literal altar; yours will be figurative—an altar of the will. In the case of some, this sacrifice is more difficult than going without food or shelter. To give up someone we love often feels like the most senseless sacrifice of all, which only intensifies the pain.

A. W. Tozer wrote about this struggle in his fine book *The Pursuit of God:*

We're often hindered from giving up our treasures to the Lord out of fear for their safety. This is especially true when our treasures are loved ones, relatives, and friends. But we need have no such fears. Our Lord came not to destroy but to save. Everything is safe which we commit to Him, and nothing is really safe which is not so committed....

Let us never forget that a truth such as this cannot be learned by rote as one would learn the facts of physical science. It must be *experienced* before we can really know them. We must, in our hearts, live through Abraham's harsh and bitter experiences if we would know the blessedness which follows them. The ancient curse will not go out painlessly; the tough, old miser within us will not lie down and die in obedience to our command. . . . He must be expelled from our soul by violence as Christ expelled the money-changers from the temple. And we shall need to steel ourselves against his piteous begging, and to recognize it as springing out of self-pity, one of the most reprehensible sins of the human heart.[3]

Perhaps you have had a relationship with an individual, and your relationship with God has declined. Still you cling, hoping it will get better. It doesn't, and it won't. God may be saying to you, "Choose Me. Sacrifice her. Sacrifice him."

You may have been in a long-term relationship with someone, and your partner has walked away . . . he or she wants nothing to do with you. God may be saying to you, "You have done all you can do. Let that person go. Let Me have that now-broken relationship as an act of worship."

You may be clinging to one of your adult children. She is moving in a direction that's not your plan. Or maybe you're afraid that she will do just fine without you. Either way, let her go. The word is *sacrifice*.

God will provide!

FINANCIAL SACRIFICE

Personal sacrifice overcomes a love for self that may be nurtured by any number of things, material wealth being only one of them. Financial sacrifice overcomes a love for money and possessions. In my own experience this is probably the easiest of the three to address. When one adequately deals with personal sacrifice and relational sacrifice, financial sacrifices naturally follow. By the time one has worked through the issues of personal treasures and idolatrous relationships, money becomes so insignificant!

Paul's letter to the church in Philippi—a letter from an itinerant preacher to a new and growing church—is a very sweet note over-flowing with joy and thanksgiving. These brothers and sisters loved Paul and believed in his ministry, and they lived to give. Overflowing with feelings of gratitude, Paul writes to them:

> You yourselves also know, Philippians, that at the first preaching of the gospel, after I left Macedonia, no church shared with me in the matter of giving and receiving but you alone; for even in Thessalonica you sent a gift more than once for my needs. Not that I seek the gift itself, but I seek for the profit which increases to your account. But I have received everything in full and have an abundance; I am amply supplied, having received from Epaphroditus what you have sent, a fragrant aroma, an acceptable sacrifice, well-pleasing to God.
>
> —PHILIPPIANS 4:15–18

From verse 15, we discover that this church was *the only one* to give. Verse 16 tells us that they gave *repeatedly*. We know from verse 18 that they gave *recently* and *generously*. Paul put his finger on the word that best describes such liberal giving on the part of the Philippians: *sacrifice*.

Notice also the follow-up promise Paul set forth in verse 19: "And my God will supply all your needs according to His riches in glory in Christ Jesus."

Their part was repeated generosity. God's part was abundantly supplying their need.

The great fear in financial sacrifice is that we might run out of provisions. We're tempted to think that giving them away will only bring the poverty sooner. Fortunately, as with relationships, God will provide. He is infinite in His resources and in His creativity. He never runs dry or shy of ideas.

WARNINGS

The discipline of sacrifice will not be easy to exercise. In addition to the loss of what you sacrifice, you will encounter a few additional trials. I want to be completely candid. This will not be easy. Maybe by knowing a few things to watch for, you'll be better equipped to sacrifice without fear.

YOUR ADVERSARY

Satan hates when people put God above all. He absolutely despises the Son of God, so the discipline that exemplifies Him will be one that the devil will do his best to undo. As soon as you put this book down, I can almost guarantee you'll be met with a decision. Weigh it carefully. Your adversary knows the power of the immediate and will try to convince you that procrastinating isn't really denying God. Don't believe it!

YOUR ACQUAINTANCES

Second, your acquaintances will think you have lost your senses. When you don't toe the line for more stuff like the rest of the crowd, they'll wonder what happened to you. I can hear it now. "Found religion, eh? Why are you giving this away? I remember a time when it meant the world to you. No need to get so fanatical!"

YOUR MIND

Third, your mind will play tricks on you, suggesting thoughts like, *If I keep sacrificing, I'll later regret losing what I did . . . and I'll eventually run out.* Panic in unguarded moments will make you feel like a fool.

YOUR FLESH

Fourth, your discipline will be tested repeatedly because the flesh seeks whatever will make itself feel safe and comfortable. Remember Tozer's vivid warning: the old miser doesn't die easily. Rather than face down the flesh on your own—it's a losing battle—stand firm in the Spirit. No need to go off donating everything you own in a foolish test of wills, yours against that of the flesh. The battle is the Lord's. Give it to Him as you exercise all of the disciplines.

Elisabeth Elliot's book introduced me to the discipline of sacrifice that dark, damp night when everything seemed so bleak. I began a journey that would teach me what it meant to be a living sacrifice. In my naiveté, I had assumed that being a living sacrifice meant having a willingness to lay down my life for Christ in one grand gesture, much as those five missionaries had done. As a marine, I had already considered the possibility of dying for my country. I felt sure I would die for Christ if circumstances demanded it. But her book showed me so much more. She writes in the 1958 epilogue of *Through Gates of Splendor:*

> We know that it was no accident. God performs all things according to the counsel of His own will. The real issues at stake on January 8, 1956, were very far greater than those which immediately involved five young men and their families, or this small tribe of naked

"savages." Letters from many countries have told of God's dealings with hundreds of men and women, through the examples of five who believed literally that "the world passeth away, and the lust thereof: but he that doeth the will of God abideth for ever."[4]

These men didn't go on a suicide mission. Their goal was not to die. Their death was the result of living a habitual life of sacrifice to Christ. Their precious lives ended in tragedy near a river in the Ecuadorian interior in the early days of 1956. They were no fools. They were heroes of the life of faith. Their deaths taught me what it meant to live. Really live.

God will not likely expect you to surrender your life all at once as these men did. Instead, He patiently waits for you to sacrifice yourself in small amounts, one decision at a time, one day at a time, so that you might enjoy an ever-increasing intimacy with Him. And this deepening intimacy with Him will inevitably make you more like Christ.

Endnotes

Introduction—The Gymnasium of the Soul
1. Kittel, Gerhard, Gerhard Friedrich, and Geoffrey William Bromiley. *Theological Dictionary of the New Testament.* Translation of: Theologisches Worterbuch Zum Neuen Testament, Page 1012. Grand Rapids, Mich.: W. B. Eerdmans, 1995 © 1985.

Chapter 1—Intimacy: Deepening Our Lives
1. Eugene Peterson, *Run with the Horses* (Downers Grove, Ill.: InterVarsity Press, 1983), p. 16.
2. A. T. Robertson, *Word Pictures in the New Testament* (Grand Rapids, Mich.: Baker, 1933), 299.
3. John R. W. Stott, *What Christ Thinks of the Church: Expository Addresses on the First Three Chapters of the Book of Revelation* (Colorado Springs: Harold Shaw, 1990), 21.
4. Ibid., 22
5. Ibid., 23
6. Isaac Watts, "Am I a Soldier of the Cross?"
7. Henri J. M. Nouwen, *The Way of the Heart: Desert Spirituality and Contemporary Ministry* (New York: Seabury, 1981), 45–46.
8. Dallas Willard, *The Spirit of the Disciplines: Understanding How God Changes Lives* (San Francisco: Harper & Row, 1988), ix–xi. Reprinted by permission of HarperCollins Publishers Inc.
9. Richard J. Foster, *Celebration of Discipline: The Path to Spiritual Growth* (San Francisco: Harper & Row, 1978), 1.

Endnotes

Chapter 2—Simplicity: Uncluttering Our Minds

1. Brief text as submitted from *The Gulag Archipelago* 1918–1956, abridged by Aleksandr I. Solzhenitsyn. Parts I–IV translated by Thomas P. Whitney. Parts V–VII translated by Harry Willetts. Abridged by Edward E. Ericson, Jr. Copyright © 1985 by the Russian Social Fund. Reprinted by permission of HarperCollins Publishers Inc.

2. Henry David Thoreau, *Walden* (Hungary: Konemann Publishers, 1996), 82–83.

3. Alfred Plummer, *A Critical and Exegetical Commentary to the Second Epistle of St. Paul to the Corinthians* (Edinburgh: T. & T. Clark, 1915), 296.

4. Alan Redpath, *Blessings Out of Buffetings: Studies in II Corinthians* (Westwood, NJ: Fleming H. Revell, 1965), 187.

5. Ibid., 187–188.

6. "Coming Home," from *On the Road with Charles Kuralt* by Charles Kuralt, copyright © 1985 by CBS Inc. Used by permission of G. P. Putnam's Sons, a division of Penguin Group (USA) Inc.

Chapter 3—Silence and Solitude: Slowing Our Pace

1. A. W. Tozer, *The Divine Conquest* (Camp Hill, Penn.: Christian Publications, 1950; copyright renewed 1978, Lowell Tozer), p. 22.

2. H.V.F. Winstone, *Howard Carter and The Discovery of the Tomb of Tutankhamen* (London: Constable and Company, 1991), 142.

3. James Moffatt, *A New Translation of the Bible Containing the Old and New Testaments,* Proverbs 2:5 (New York: Harper & Brothers, 1954), 701.

4. Edwin Hodder, "Thy Word is Like a Garden, Lord," Public Domain.

5. Philip Schaff, *History of the Christian Church,* Vol. VII (Grand Rapids, Mich.: Eerdmans, 1950), 502.

6. Robert Laird Harris, Leason Leonard Archer, and Bruce K. Waltke, *Theological Wordbook of the Old Testament* (Chicago: Moody, 1980), 2198.

7. Ron Mehl, *What God Whispers in the Night* (Sisters, Ore.: Multnomah, 2000), 97.

8. Henri J. M. Nouwen, *The Way of the Heart: Desert Spirituality and Contemporary Ministry* (San Francisco: HarperCollins, 1981), 58.

9. Ibid., 59.

10. Ibid., 64.

11. Ibid., 65.

12. Taken from "New Bible Commentary" edited by Gordon J. Wenham, J. Alec Motyer, Donald A. Carson and R.T. France. Copyright(c)1970 Inter-Varsity Press, UK. Used with permission of InterVarsity Press, P.O. Box 1400, Downers Grove, IL 60515. www.ivpress.com.

13. Robert Laird Harris, *Theological Wordbook of the Old Testament,* 193.

14.   Merriam-Webster, Inc. *Merriam-Webster's Collegiate Dictionary*. 10th Ed. (Springfield, Mass.: Merriam-Webster, 1996), s.v. "journal."

Chapter 4—Surrender: Releasing Our Grip
1.   William Hendriksen, *Philippians* (Grand Rapids, Mich.: 1962), 100.
2.   Arthur Bennett, ed., *The Valley of Vision: A Collection of Puritan Prayers and Devotions* (Carlisle, Penn.: The Banner of Truth Trust, 1975), 91.
3.   Helen H. Lemmel, "Turn Your Eyes Upon Jesus," Brentwood Benson Music(c)1950.
4.   Reprinted from *The Pursuit of God* by A. W. Tozer, copyright (c)1982, 1993 by Christian Publications, Inc. Used by permission of Christian Publications, Inc., 800.233.4443, www.christianpublications.com.
5.   Wyatt Prunty, "Learning the Bicycle" (for Heather), *The American Scholar*, 58, No. 1 (Winter 1989):122.
6.   Catherine Marshall, ed., *The Best of Peter Marshall* (Grand Rapids, Mich.: Chosen Books, a division of Baker, 1983), 141.

Chapter 5—Prayer: Calling Out
1.   Richard J. Foster and James Bryan Smith, ed., *Devotional Classics* (San Francisco: Harper, 1993), 103.
2.   E. M. Bounds, *The Complete Works of E. M. Bounds on Prayer* (Grand Rapids, Mich.: 1990), 93.
3.   Richard J. Foster, *Devotional Classics*, 89.
4.   Ben Patterson, *Deepening Your Conversation with God* (Minneapolis: Bethany House, 1999), 22.
5.   Dallas Willard, *The Spirit of the Disciplines: Understanding How God Changes Lives* (San Francisco: Harper & Row, 1988), 185-86. Reprinted by permission of HarperCollins Inc.
6.   R. Kent Hughes, *Disciplines of a Godly Man* (Wheaton, Ill.: Crossway, 1991), 105. Used by permission. www.gnpcb.org.
7.   Richard J. Foster, *Devotional Classics*, 134.
8.   Ibid., 137.

Chapter 6—Humility: Bowing Low
1.   Dallas Willard, *The Spirit of the Disciplines: Understanding How God Changes Lives* (San Francisco: Harper & Row, 1988), 3–4. Reprinted by permission of HarperCollins Inc.
2.   Philip Yancey and Dr. Paul Brand, *In the Likeness of God* (Grand Rapids, Mich.: Zondervan, 2004), 15.
3.   J. Steven Wilkins, *Call of Duty: The Sterling Nobility of Robert E. Lee* (Nashville: Cumberland House, 1996), 244.

Endnotes

4. William Barclay, *The Gospel of Mark* (Philadelphia: Westminster Press, 1956), 267.
5. Rudyard Kipling, *Rudyard Kipling Complete Verse* (New York: Doubleday, 1940), 370.
6. Kenneth S. Davis, *Soldier of Democracy* (New York: Doubleday, 1945), 543.

Chapter 7—Self-Control: Holding Back

1. Fritz Ridenour, *How to Be a Christian Without Being Religious* (Minneapolis: Billy Graham Association, 1967), 55.
2. Sun Tzu, *The Art of War* (New York: Doubleday, 1988), 18.
3. Charlie Peacock, "In the Light," ©1991 Sparrow Song. All Rights Reserved. International copyright secured. Used by Permission.
4. Maxie Dunham, *The Communicator's Commentary*, vol. 8 (Dallas: Word, 1982), 120. All rights reserved.
5. Richard J. Foster, *The Challenge of the Disciplined Life: Christian Reflections on Money, Sex, and Power* (New York: HarperCollins, 1985), 203. Reprinted by permission of HarperCollins Publishers Inc.

Chapter 8—Sacrifice: Giving Over

1. Richard J. Foster, *The Challenge of the Disciplined Life: Christian Reflections on Money, Sex, and Power* (New York: HarperCollins, 1985), 61–2. Reprinted by permission of HarperCollins Publishers Inc.
2. Dallas Willard, *The Spirit of the Disciplines: Understanding How God Changes Lives* (San Francisco: Harper & Row, 1988), 175. Reprinted by permission of HarperCollins Inc.
3. Reprinted from *The Pursuit of God* by A. W. Tozer, copyright (c)1982, 1993 by Christian Publications, Inc. Used by permission of Christian Publications, Inc., 800.233.4443, www.christianpublications.com.
4. Elisabeth Elliot, *Through Gates of Splendor* (Carol Stream, Ill.: Tyndale, 1981), 259.